of Address

Titles and Forms of Address

A guide to correct use

Twenty-second edition

A & C Black • London

Twenty-second edition published 2007
A & C Black Publishers Limited
38 Soho Square
London W1D 3HB
www.acblack.com

© 2007 A & C Black Publishers Limited

ISBN 978-0-7136-8325-7

A CIP catalogue record for this book is available from the British Library.

First edition 1918	Twelfth edition 1964
Second edition 1929	Thirteenth edition 1968
Third edition 1932	Fourteenth edition 1971
Fourth edition 1936	Fifteenth edition 1976
Fifth edition 1939	Sixteenth edition 1978
Sixth edition 1945	Seventeenth edition 1980
Seventh edition 1949	Eighteenth edition 1985
Eighth edition 1951	Nineteenth edition 1990
Ninth edition 1955	Twentieth edition 1997
Tenth edition 1958	Twenty-first edition 2002
Eleventh edition 1961	

This book is produced using paper that is made from wood grown in managed, sustainable forests. It is natural, renewable and recyclable. The logging and manufacturing processes conform to the environmental regulations of the country of origin.

Typeset in 10/11pt Times

Printed and bound in Great Britain by
CPI Cox & Wyman, Reading, RG1 8EX

Foreword

The correct use of titles, and other distinguishing marks of honour or of office, has generally become established over a long period through the usage followed by the title-holders themselves and by those associated with them. Similarly, and very gradually, there occur modifications and changes in practice.

It seems desirable to point out that while great formality may from time to time be appropriate, and the forms to be used in such cases are therefore given, it will more often be proper – and more usual – to use simpler forms, as indicated throughout, in ordinary correspondence whether business or social.

In view of security risks, it is wise to enquire in advance how envelopes should be addressed to people at home. If that is not possible, omit title, office and rank, unless advised otherwise by the recipient. This precaution obviously relates particularly to members of the armed forces, the police and legal officers (from judges to members of the prison service).

It should be made clear that etiquette is a different subject and is not touched upon in this book.

The publishers are grateful to correspondents who have kindly suggested additions and improvements. At the same time they are bound to say that they are unable to provide an advisory or information service.

2007

Contents

Abbreviations

This list consists solely of abbreviations which may be used after the name. These fall into two groups:

they require forms of address described in the text of this book;

they are fellowships or similar qualifications which would be used only in a professional context.

Pages 163–68 give the rules by which the order of the various categories is determined.

The selection is restricted to the above two groups because so many initials and acronyms are now in use. For fuller and more comprehensive information readers are referred to:

Who's Who
pub. yearly by A & C Black

Oxford Dictionary of Abbreviations
2nd edn 1998, OUP
in libraries or electronically

New Penguin Dictionary of Abbreviations
2000, Penguin
in libraries

A

AA	Augustinians of the Assumption
AB	Bachelor of Arts (US)
AC	Companion of the Order of Australia
AD	Dame of the Order of Australia
ADC	Aide-de-camp
AE	Air Efficiency Award
AEM	Air Efficiency Medal
AFC	Air Force Cross
AFM	Air Force Medal
AK	Knight of the Order of Australia
AM	Albert Medal; Member of the Order of Australia
AO	Officer of the Order of Australia
AOE	Alberta Order of Excellence (Canada)
ARA	Associate, Royal Academy
ARRC	Associate, Royal Red Cross

B

BA	Bachelor of Arts
Bart or **Bt**	Baronet
BCL	Bachelor of Civil Law
BD	Bachelor of Divinity
BEM	British Empire Medal
BLitt	Bachelor of Letters
BM	Bachelor of Medicine
BMus	Bachelor of Music
BSc	Bachelor of Science
BSM	Barbados Service Medal
BSS	Barbados Service Star
Bt	Baronet
Btss	Baronetess

C

CA	Chartered Accountant (Scotland)
CB	Companion of the Order of the Bath
CBE	Commander of the Order of the British Empire
CBiol	Chartered Biologist

CC	Companion of the Order of Canada
CChem	Chartered Chemist
CD	Canadian Forces Decoration
CEng	Chartered Engineer
CF	Chaplain to the Forces
CGA	Community of the Glorious Ascension
CGM	Conspicuous Gallantry Medal
CH	Companion of Honour
CHB	Companion of Honour of Barbados
CI	Imperial Order of the Crown of India
CIE	Companion of the Order of the Indian Empire
CJM	Congregation of Jesus and Mary (Eudist Fathers)
CM	Member of the Order of Canada; Congregation of the Mission (Vincentians); Master in Surgery; Certificated Master
CMG	Companion of the Order of St Michael and St George
CMM	Commander, Order of Military Merit (Canada)
CNZM	Companion of the Order of Merit (NZ)
CPA	Chartered Patent Agent
CPhys	Chartered Physicist
CPM	Colonial Police Medal
CPsychol	Chartered Psychologist
CQ	Chevalier de l'ordre national du Québec (Canada)
CR	Community of the Resurrection
CSC	Conspicuous Service Cross; Congregation of the Holy Cross
CSI	Companion of the Order of the Star of India
CSSp	Holy Ghost Father
CSSR	Congregation of the Most Holy Redeemer (Redemptorist Order)
CText	Chartered Textile Technologist
CV	Cross of Valour (Canada)
CVO	Commander of the Royal Victorian Order

D

DA	Dame of St Andrew
DAgr	Doctor of Agriculture
DAppSc	Doctor of Applied Science
DASc	Doctor in Agricultural Sciences

DBA	Doctor of Business Administration
DBE	Dame Commander of the Order of the British Empire
DCB	Dame Commander of the Order of the Bath
DCh	Doctor of Surgery
DCL	Doctor of Civil Law
DCM	Distinguished Conduct Medal
DCMG	Dame Commander of the Order of St Michael and St George
DCnL	Doctor of Canon Law
DCS	Doctor of Commercial Sciences
DCVO	Dame Commander of Royal Victorian Order
DD	Doctor of Divinity
DDS	Doctor of Dental Surgery
DDSc	Doctor of Dental Science
DE	Doctor of Engineering
DEconSc	Doctor of Economic Science
DEd	Doctor of Education
DEng	Doctor of Engineering
DFA	Doctor of Fine Arts
DFC	Distinguished Flying Cross
DFM	Distinguished Flying Medal
DHL	Doctor of Humane Letters; Doctor of Hebrew Literature
DJur	*Doctor Juris*
DL	Deputy Lieutenant
DLitt or **DLit**	Doctor of Literature; Doctor of Letters
DM	Doctor of Medicine
DMet	Doctor of Metallurgy
DMus	Doctor of Music
DNZM	Dame Grand Companion of the Order of Merit (NZ)
DO	Doctor of Osteopathy
DPhil	Doctor of Philosophy
DœEcPol	Doctor Œconomiæ Politicæ
DSC	Distinguished Service Cross
DSc	Doctor of Science
DScMil	Doctor of Military Science
DSM	Distinguished Service Medal
DSO	Companion of the Distinguished Service Order
DSocSc	Doctor of Social Science
DStJ	Dame of the Venerable Order of St John of Jerusalem
DTech	Doctor of Technology

DTheol	Doctor of Theology
DVM	Doctor of Veterinary Medicine
DVMS	Doctor of Veterinary Medicine and Surgery
DVSc	Doctor of Veterinary Science

E

ED	Efficiency Decoration; Doctor of Engineering (US)
EdB	Bachelor of Education
EdD	Doctor of Education
EM	Edward Medal
ERD	Emergency Reserve Decoration (Army)
Esq	Esquire
EurIng	European Engineer

F

FAMS	Fellow, Ancient Monuments Society
FArborA	Fellow, Arboricultural Association
FAS	Fellow, Antiquarian Society
FASI	Fellow, Architects' and Surveyors' Institute
FBA	Fellow, British Academy
FBCO	Fellow, British College of Ophthalmologists
FBCS	Fellow, British Computer Society
FBHI	Fellow, British Horological Institute
FBHS	Fellow, British Horse Society
FBIBA	Fellow, British Insurance Brokers' Association
FBID	Fellow, British Institute of Interior Design
FBIPP	Fellow, British Institute of Professional Photography
FBIRA	Fellow, British Institute of Regulatory Affairs
FBIS	Fellow, British Interplanetary Society
FBKSTS	Fellow, British Kinematograph, Sound and Television Society
FBOA	Fellow, British Optical Association
FBOU	Fellow, British Ornithologists' Union
FBPsS	Fellow, British Psychological Society
FBSM	Fellow, Birmingham School of Music
FCA	Fellow, Institute of Chartered Accountants
FCAM	Fellow, CAM Foundation
FCAnaesth	Fellow, College of Anaesthetists

FCBSI	Fellow, Chartered Building Societies Institute
FCCA	Fellow, Association of Certified Accountants
FCCEA	Fellow, Commonwealth Council for Educational Administration
FCCS	Fellow, Corporation of Secretaries
FCFI	Fellow, Clothing and Footwear Institute
FCGI	Fellow, City and Guilds of London Institute
FCH	Fellow, Coopers Hill College
FChS	Fellow, Society of Chiropodists
FCI	Fellow, Institute of Commerce
FCIA	Fellow, Corporation of Insurance Agents
FCIArb	Fellow, Chartered Institute of Arbitrators
FCIB	Fellow, Corporation of Insurance Brokers; Fellow, Chartered Institute of Bankers
FCIBSE	Fellow, Chartered Institution of Building Services Engineers
FCII	Fellow, Chartered Insurance Institute
FCIM	Fellow, Chartered Institute of Marketing
FCIOB	Fellow, Chartered Institute of Building
FCIS	Fellow, Institute of Chartered Secretaries and Administrators
FCIT	Fellow, Chartered Institute of Transport
FCIWEM	Fellow, Chartered Institution of Water and Environmental Management
FCMA	Fellow, Institute of Cost and Management Accountants
FCOphth	Fellow, College of Ophthalmogists
FCP	Fellow, College of Preceptors
FCPS	Fellow, College of Physicians and Surgeons
FCSD	Fellow, Chartered Society of Designers
FCSP	Fellow, Chartered Society of Physiotherapy
FCST	Fellow, College of Speech Therapists
FCT	Fellow, Association of Corporate Treasurers
FCTB	Fellow, College of Teachers of the Blind
FDS	Fellow in Dental Surgery
FDSRCPS Glas	Fellow in Dental Surgery, Royal College of Physicians and Surgeons of Glasgow
FDSRCS	Fellow in Dental Surgery, Royal College of Surgeons of England
FDSRCSE	Fellow in Dental Surgery, Royal College of Surgeons of Edinburgh
FEIS	Fellow, Educational Institute of Scotland
FEng	Fellow, Fellowship of Engineering

FES	Fellow, Entomological Society; Fellow, Ethnological Society
FFA	Fellow, Faculty of Actuaries (in Scotland); Fellow, Institute of Financial Accountants
FFARCSI	Fellow, Faculty of Anaesthetists, Royal College of Surgeons in Ireland
FFB	Fellow, Faculty of Building
FFDRCSI	Fellow, Faculty of Dentistry, Royal College of Surgeons in Ireland
FFHom	Fellow, Faculty of Homeopathy
FFOM	Fellow, Faculty of Occupational Medicine
FFPath, RCPI	Fellow, Faculty of Pathologists of the Royal College of Physicians of Ireland
FFPHM	Fellow, Faculty of Public Health Medicine
FGA	Fellow, Gemmological Association
FGCM	Fellow, Guild of Church Musicians
FGGE	Fellow, Guild of Glass Engineers
FGI	Fellow, Institute of Certificated Grocers
FGS	Fellow, Geological Society
FGSM	Fellow, Guildhall School of Music and Drama
FGSM(MT)	Fellow, Guildhall School of Music and Drama (Music Therapy)
FHAS	Fellow, Highland and Agricultural Society of Scotland
FHCIMA	Fellow, Hotel Catering and Institutional Management Association
FHFS	Fellow, Human Factors Society
FHS	Fellow, Heraldry Society
FH-WC	Fellow, Heriot-Watt College (now University), Edinburgh
FIA	Fellow, Institute of Actuaries
FIAA&S	Fellow, Incorporated Association of Architects and Surveyors
FIAgrE	Fellow, Institution of Agricultural Engineers
FIAI	Fellow, Institute of Industrial and Commercial Accountants
FIAL	Fellow, International Institute of Arts and Letters
FIAM	Fellow, International Academy of Management
FInstAM	Fellow, Institute of Administrative Management
FIAP	Fellow, Institution of Analysts and Programmers
FIAWS	Fellow, International Academy of Wood Sciences
FIBD	Fellow, Institute of British Decorators

FIBiol	Fellow, Institute of Biology
FIBiotech	Fellow, Institute for Biotechnical Studies
FIBP	Fellow, Institute of British Photographers
FIBScot	Fellow, Institute of Bankers in Scotland
FIC	Fellow, Imperial College
FICAI	Fellow, Institute of Chartered Accountants in Ireland
FICD	Fellow, Institute of Civil Defence
FICE	Fellow, Institution of Civil Engineers
FICeram	Fellow, Institute of Ceramics
FICFor	Fellow, Institute of Chartered Foresters
FIChemE	Fellow, Institution of Chemical Engineers
FICI	Fellow, Institute of Chemistry of Ireland
FICM	Fellow, Institute of Credit Management
FICMA	Fellow, Institute of Cost and Management Accountants
FICorrST	Fellow, Institution of Corrosion Science and Technology
FICS	Fellow, Institute of Chartered Shipbrokers; Fellow, International College of Surgeons
FICT	Fellow, Institute of Concrete Technologists
FICW	Fellow, Institute of Clerks of Works of Great Britain
FIDE	Fellow, Institute of Design Engineers
FIEC	Fellow, Institute of Employment Consultants
FIED	Fellow, Institution of Engineering Designers
FIEE	Fellow, Institution of Electrical Engineers
FIEx	Fellow, Institute of Export
FIExpE	Fellow, Institute of Explosives Engineers
FIEIE	Fellow, Institution of Electronics and Electrical Incorporated Engineers
FIFF	Fellow, Institute of Freight Forwarders
FIFM	Fellow, Institute of Fisheries Management
FIFST	Fellow, Institute of Food Science and Technology
FIGasE	Fellow, Institution of Gas Engineers
FIGCM	Fellow, Incorporated Guild of Church Musicians
FIGD	Fellow, Institute of Grocery Distribution
FIH	Fellow, Institute of Housing; Fellow, Institute of the Horse
FIHE	Fellow, Institute of Health Education
FIHort	Fellow, Institute of Horticulture
FIHospE	Fellow, Institute of Hospital Engineering

FIHT	Fellow, Institution of Highways and Transportation
FIIC	Fellow, International Institute for Conservation of Historic and Artistic Works
FIIM	Fellow, Institution of Industrial Managers
FIInfSc	Fellow, Institute of Information Scientists
FIInst	Fellow, Imperial Institute
FIL	Fellow, Institute of Linguists
FILDM	Fellow, Institute of Logistics and Distribution Management
FIM	Fellow, Institute of Materials
FIMA	Fellow, Institute of Mathematics and its Applications
FIMarE	Fellow, Institute of Marine Engineers
FIMC	Fellow, Institute of Management Consultants
FIMECHE	Fellow, Institution of Mechanical Engineers
FIMFT	Fellow, Institute of Maxillo-facial Technology
FIMGTechE	Fellow, Institution of Mechanical and General Technician Engineers
FIMH	Fellow, Institute of Materials Handling; Fellow, Institute of Military History
FIMI	Fellow, Institute of the Motor Industry
FIMinE	Fellow, Institution of Mining Engineers
FIMIT	Fellow, Institute of Musical Instrument Technology
FIMLS	Fellow, Institute of Medical Laboratory Sciences
FIMM	Fellow, Institute of Mining and Metallurgy
FIMS	Fellow, Institute of Mathematical Statistics
FInstAM	Fellow, Institute of Administrative Management
FIinstB	Fellow, Institution of Buyers
FInstD	Fellow, Institute of Directors
FInstE	Fellow, Institute of Energy
FInstFF	Fellow, Institute of Freight Forwarders Ltd
FInstLEx	Fellow, Institute of Legal Executives
FInstM	Fellow, Institute of Meat
FInstMC	Fellow, Institute of Measurement and Control
FInstP	Fellow, Institute of Physics
FInstPet	Fellow, Institute of Petroleum
FInstPI	Fellow, Institute of Patentees and Inventors
FInstPS	Fellow, Institute of Purchasing and Supply
FInstSMM	Fellow, Institute of Sales and Marketing Management
FINucE	Fellow, Institution of Nuclear Engineers
FIOA	Fellow, Institute of Acoustics
FIOP	Fellow, Institute of Printing

FIPA	Fellow, Institute of Practitioners in Advertising
FIPG	Fellow, Institute of Professional Goldsmiths
FIPR	Fellow, Institute of Public Relations
FIProdE	Fellow, Institution of Production Engineers
FIQ	Fellow, Institute of Quarrying
FIQA	Fellow, Institute of Quality Assurance
FIQPS	Fellow, Institute of Qualified Private Secretaries
FIQS	Fellow, Institute of Quantity Surveyors
FIRSE	Fellow, Institute of Railway Signalling Engineers
FIRTE	Fellow, Institute of Road Transport Engineers
FIS	Fellow, Institute of Statisticians
FISA	Fellow, Incorporated Secretaries' Association
FISE	Fellow, Institution of Sales Engineers; Fellow, Institution of Sanitary Engineers
FIST	Fellow, Institute of Science Technology
FISTC	Fellow, Institute of Scientific and Technical Communicators
FIStructE	Fellow, Institution of Structural Engineers
FISW	Fellow, Institute of Social Work
FITD	Fellow, Institute of Training and Development
FITE	Fellow, Institution of Electrical and Electronics Technician Engineers
FIWSc	Fellow, Institute of Wood Science
FJI	Fellow, Institute of Journalists
FKC	Fellow, King's College London
FKCHMS	Fellow, King's College Hospital Medical School
FLA	Fellow, Library Association
FLAI	Fellow, Library Association of Ireland
FLCM	Fellow, London College of Music
FLHS	Fellow, London Historical Society
FLI	Fellow, Landscape Institute
FLIA	Fellow, Life Insurance Association
FLS	Fellow, Linnean Society
FMA	Fellow, Museums Association
FMES	Fellow, Minerals Engineering Society
FMS	Fellow, Institute of Management Services; Fellow, Medical Society
FNAEA	Fellow, National Association of Estate Agents
FNECInst	Fellow, North East Coast Institution of Engineers and Shipbuilders
FNI	Fellow, Nautical Institute
FOR	Fellowship of Operational Research

FPEA	Fellow, Physical Education Association
FPhS	Fellow, Philosophical Society of England
FPMI	Fellow, Pensions Management Institute
FPRI	Fellow, Plastics and Rubber Institute
FPhysS	Fellow, Physical Society
FRA	Fellow, Royal Academy
FRAD	Fellow, Royal Academy of Dancing
FRAeS	Fellow, Royal Aeronautical Society
FRAgS	Fellow, Royal Agricultural Societies (ie of England, Scotland and Wales)
FRAI	Fellow, Royal Anthropological Institute
FRAM	Fellow, Royal Academy of Music
FRAS	Fellow, Royal Astronomical Society; Fellow, Royal Asiatic Society
FRASE	Fellow, Royal Agricultural Society of England
FRBS	Fellow, Royal Society of British Sculptors
FRCGP	Fellow, Royal College of General Practitioners
FRCM	Fellow, Royal College of Music
FRCN	Fellow, Royal College of Nursing
FRCO	Fellow, Royal College of Organists
FRCO(CHM)	Fellow, Royal College of Organists with Diploma in Choir Training
FRCOG	Fellow, Royal College of Obstetricians and Gynaecologists
FRCP	Fellow, Royal College of Physicians, London
FRCPath	Fellow, Royal College of Pathologists
FRCPE and **FRCPEd**	Fellow, Royal College of Physicians, Edinburgh
FRCPGlas	Fellow, Royal College of Physicians and Surgeons of Glasgow
FRCPI	Fellow, Royal College of Physicians of Ireland
FRCPsych	Fellow, Royal College of Psychiatrists
FRCR	Fellow, Royal College of Radiologists
FRCS	Fellow, Royal College of Surgeons of England
FRCSE and **FRCSEd**	Fellow, Royal College of Surgeons of Edinburgh
FRCSGlas	Fellow, Royal College of Physicians and Surgeons of Glasgow
FRCSI	Fellow, Royal College of Surgeons in Ireland
FRCSoc	Fellow, Royal Commonwealth Society
FRCVS	Fellow, Royal College of Veterinary Surgeons
FREconS	Fellow, Royal Economic Society

FRES	Fellow, Royal Entomological Society of London
FRGS	Fellow, Royal Geographical Society
FRHistS	Fellow, Royal Historical Society
FRHS	Fellow, Royal Horticultural Society
FRIAS	Fellow, Royal Incorporation of Architects of Scotland
FRIBA	Fellow, Royal Institute of British Architects
FRICS	Fellow, Royal Institution of Chartered Surveyors
FRIN	Fellow, Royal Institute of Navigation
FRINA	Fellow, Royal Institution of Naval Architects
FRIPHH	Fellow, Royal Institute of Public Health and Hygiene
FRMCM	Fellow, Royal Manchester College of Music
FRMedSoc	Fellow, Royal Medical Society
FRMetS	Fellow, Royal Meteorological Society
FRMS	Fellow, Royal Microscopical Society
FRNCM	Fellow, Royal Northern College of Music
FRNS	Fellow, Royal Numismatic Society
FRPharmS	Fellow, Royal Pharmaceutical Society
FRPS	Fellow, Royal Photographic Society
FRPSL	Fellow, Royal Philatelic Society, London
FRS	Fellow, Royal Society
FRSAI	Fellow, Royal Society of Antiquaries of Ireland
FRSAMD	Fellow, Royal Scottish Academy of Music and Drama
FRSC	Fellow, Royal Society of Chemistry
FRSCM	Fellow, Royal School of Church Music
FRSE	Fellow, Royal Society of Edinburgh
FRSGS	Fellow, Royal Scottish Geographical Society
FRSH	Fellow, Royal Society for the Promotion of Health
FRSL	Fellow, Royal Society of Literature
FRST	Fellow, Royal Society of Teachers
FRSTM&H	Fellow, Royal Society of Tropical Medicine and Hygiene
FRTPI	Fellow, Royal Town Planning Institute
FRTS	Fellow, Royal Television Society
FRVA	Fellow, Rating and Valuation Association
FRVC	Fellow, Royal Veterinary College
FRVIA	Fellow, Royal Victorian Institute of Architects
FRZSScot	Fellow, Royal Zoological Society of Scotland
FSA	Fellow, Society of Antiquaries

FSAA	Fellow, Society of Incorporated Accountants and Auditors
FSAE	Fellow, Society of Automotive Engineers; Fellow, Society of Art Education
FSAM	Fellow, Society of Art Masters
FSAScot	Fellow, Society of Antiquaries of Scotland
FSBI	Fellow, Savings Banks Institute
FSCA	Fellow, Society of Company and Commercial Accountants
FSDC	Fellow, Society of Dyers and Colourists
FSE	Fellow, Society of Engineers
FSG	Fellow, Society of Genealogists
FSGT	Fellow, Society of Glass Technology
FSLAET	Fellow, Society of Licensed Aircraft Engineers and Technologists
FSLTC	Fellow, Society of Leather Technologists and Chemists
FSRHE	Fellow, Society for Research into Higher Education
FSS	Fellow, Royal Statistical Society
FSTD	Fellow, Society of Typographic Designers
FSVA	Fellow, Incorporated Society of Valuers and Auctioneers
FTCD	Fellow, Trinity College, Dublin
FTCL	Fellow, Trinity College of Music, London
FTI	Fellow, Textile Institute
FTII	Fellow, Institute of Taxation
FTP	Fellow, Thames Polytechnic
FUMIST	Fellow, University of Manchester Institute of Science and Technology
FWA	Fellow, World Academy of Arts and Sciences
FWeldI	Fellow, Welding Institute
FZS	Fellow, Zoological Society

G

GBE	Knight or Dame Grand Cross of the Order of the British Empire
GC	George Cross
GCB	Knight or Dame Grand Cross of the Order of the Bath

GCIE	Knight Grand Commander of the Order of the Indian Empire
GCM	Gold Crown of Merit (Barbados)
GCMG	Knight or Dame Grand Cross of the Order of St Michael and St George
GCSG	Knight Grand Cross of the Order of St Gregory the Great
GCStJ	Knight or Dame Grand Cross of the Venerable Order of St John of Jerusalem
GCSI	Knight Grand Commander of the Order of the Star of India
GCVO	Knight or Dame Grand Cross of the Royal Victorian Order
GM	George Medal
GNZM	Knight Grand Companion of the Order of Merit (NZ)
GOQ	Grand Officier de l'ordre national du Québec (Canada)

H

HM	His *or* Her Majesty; His *or* Her Majesty's

I

ISO	Imperial Service Order

J

JCD	*Juris Canonici* (or *Civilis*) *Doctor* (Doctor of Canon (or Civil) Law)
Jnr	Junior
JP	Justice of the Peace
JSD	Doctor of Juristic Science

K

KA	Knight (or Dame) of St Andrew

KBE	Knight Commander Order of the British Empire
KC	King's Counsel
KCB	Knight Commander of the Order of the Bath
KCIE	Knight Commander, Order of the Indian Empire
KCMG	Knight Commander, Order of St Michael and St George
KCSI	Knight Commander, Order of the Star of India
KCVO	Knight Commander of the Royal Victorian Order
KG	Knight of the Order of the Garter
KHC	Hon. Chaplain to the King
KHDS	Hon. Dental Surgeon to the King
KHNS	Hon. Nursing Sister to the King
KHP	Hon. Physician to the King
KHS	Hon. Surgeon to the King; Knight of the Holy Sepulchre
KM	Knight of Malta
KNZM	Knight of the Order of Merit (NZ)
KP	Knight of the Order of St Patrick
KPM	King's Police Medal
KStJ	Knight of the Venerable Order of St John of Jerusalem
KSG	Knight of the Order of St Gregory the Great
KSS	Knight of the Order of St Sylvester
KT	Knight of the Order of the Thistle
Kt	Knight

L

LG	Lady of the Order of the Garter
LitD or **LittD**	Doctor of Literature; Doctor of Letters
LLB	Bachelor of Laws
LLD	Doctor of Laws
LLM	Master of Laws
LRCP	Licentiate, Royal College of Physicians, London
LT	Lady of the Order of the Thistle
LVO	Lieutenant of the Royal Victorian Order

M

MA	Master of Arts
MBE	Member, Order of the British Empire

MC	Military Cross
MD	Doctor of Medicine
MEC	Member of Executive Council
MHA	Member of House of Assembly
MHK	Member of the House of Keys
MHR	Member of the House of Representatives
MICE	Member, Institution of Civil Engineers
MLA	Member of Legislative Assembly; Master in Landscape Architecture
MLC	Member of Legislative Council
MM	Military Medal
MMM	Member, Order of Military Merit (Canada)
MNZM	Member of the Order of Merit (NZ)
MP	Member of Parliament
MPP	Member, Provincial Parliament
MRSC	Member, Royal Society of Chemistry
MSC	Missionaries of the Sacred Heart
MSM	Meritorious Service Medal
MusBec	Bachelor of Music
MusB	Bachelor of Music
MusD	Doctor of Music
MVO	Member, Royal Victorian Order

N

NEAC	New English Art Club
NZM	New Zealand Order of Merit

O

OBC	Order of British Columbia (Canada)
OBE	Officer, Order of the British Empire
OC	Officer of the Order of Canada
OFM	Order of Friars Minor (Franciscans)
OFMCap	Order of Friars Minor Capuchin (Franciscans)
OFMConv	Order of Friars Minor Conventual (Franciscans)
OGS	Oratory of the Good Shepherd
OJ	Order of Jamaica
OM	Order of Merit
OMI	Oblate of Mary Immaculate
OMM	Officer, Order of Military Merit (Canada)

ONZ	Order of New Zealand (member)
ONZM	Officer of the Order of Merit (NZ)
OOnt	Order of Ontario (Canada)
OP	*Ordinis Praedicatorum* : of the Order of Preachers (Dominican)
OQ	Officier de l'ordre national du Québec (Canada)
OSA	Order of St Augustine (Augustinian)
OSB	Order of St Benedict (Benedictine)
OSFC	Franciscan (Capuchin) Order

P

PC	Privy Counsellor
PhD	Doctor of Philosophy
PrEng	Professional Engineer

Q

QC	Queen's Counsel
QFSM	Queen's Fire Service Medal for Distinguished Service
QGM	Queen's Gallantry Medal
QHC	Queen's Honorary Chaplain
QHDS	Queen's Honorary Dental Surgeon
QHNS	Queen's Honorary Nursing Sister
QHP	Queen's Honorary Physician
QHS	Queen's Honorary Surgeon
QPM	Queen's Police Medal
QSM	Queen's Service Medal (NZ)
QSO	Queen's Service Order (NZ)

R

RA	Royal Academician
RAF	Royal Air Force
RAM	Member Royal Academy of Music
RBA	Member Royal Society of British Artists
RCamA	Member Royal Cambrian Academy
RD	Royal Naval Reserve Decoration
RDI	Royal Designer for Industry (Royal Society of Arts)

RE	Fellow of Royal Society of Painter-Printmakers
RGN	Registered General Nurse
RHA	Royal Hibernian Academy; Royal Horse Artillery
RI	Member Royal Institute of Painters in Water Colours
RIBA	Member Royal Institute of British Architects
RM	Royal Marines
RMN	Registered Mental Nurse
RN	Royal Navy
RNT	Registered Nurse Tutor
ROI	Member Royal Institute of Oil Painters
RP	Member Royal Society of Portrait Painters
RRC	Royal Red Cross
RSA	Royal Scottish Academician
RSCN	Registered Sick Children's Nurse
RSW	Member, Royal Scottish Society of Painters in Water Colours
Rtd	Retired
RWA (RWEA)	Member, Royal West of England Academy
RWS	Member of Royal Society of Painters in Water Colours

S

SC	Star of Courage (Canada); Senior Counsel (Eire)
ScD	Doctor of Science
SCF	Senior Chaplain to the Forces
SCM	Silver Crown of Merit (Barbados); State Certified Midwife
SEN	State Enrolled Nurse
SGM	Sea Gallantry Medal
SJ	Society of Jesus (Jesuits)
SJD	Doctor of Juristic Science
SOM	Saskatchewan Order of Merit (Canada)
SOSc	Society of Ordained Scientists
SRN	State Registered Nurse
SRP	State Registered Physiotherapist
SSC	Solicitor before Supreme Court (Scotland)
SSF	Society of St Francis
SSJE	Society of St John the Evangelist
SSM	Society of the Sacred Mission

STD	*Sacrae Theologiae Doctor* (Doctor of Sacred Theology)
T	
TD	Territorial Efficiency Decoration; Efficiency Decoration (T&AVR) (since April 1967); Teachta Dala (Member of the Dáil, Eire)
ThD	Doctor of Theology
TSD	Tertiary of St Dominic
U	
UJD	*Utriusque Juris Doctor*, Doctor of both Laws (Doctor of Canon and Civil Law)
V	
VA	Royal Order of Victoria and Albert
VC	Victoria Cross
VD	Volunteer Officers' Decoration
VG	Vicar-General
VL	Vice Lord-Lieutenant
VRD	Royal Naval Volunteer Reserve Officers' Decoration
W	
WRAC	Women's Royal Army Corps
WRAF	Women's Royal Air Force
WRNS	Women's Royal Naval Service
WS	Writer to the Signet (Scotland)
Y	
yr	younger

ROYALTY

A writer not personally known to the Queen or other member of the Royal Family should address his letter to the Private Secretary, Equerry or Lady in Waiting of the person concerned, asking that the subject of the letter be made known to Her Majesty (or to His or Her Royal Highness).

The Queen

In speech

On presentation to the Queen the subject does not start the conversation. He or she will answer, using in the first instance the title Your Majesty, and subsequently Ma'am.

In writing

Letter

Madam, *or*
May it please Your Majesty,

I have the honour to remain, Madam,
Your Majesty's most humble and obedient subject,

Envelope

Formally

(For formal or State documents only)
To The Queen's Most Excellent Majesty

Otherwise

To Her Majesty The Queen

The Duke of Edinburgh

The Duke is entitled to the style of a Prince of the Blood Royal, as His Royal Highness The Prince Philip, Duke of Edinburgh.

In speech

The same rules apply as for the Queen, the title used in the first instance being Your Royal Highness, and subsequently Sir.

In writing	*Letter*

Sir,

I have the honour to be, Sir,
Your Royal Highness's most humble and obedient
servant,

In writing   *Envelope*

To His Royal Highness The Prince Philip,
Duke of Edinburgh

Princes and Princesses of the Blood Royal
Dukes and Duchesses of the Blood Royal

In speech   For all royal princes the same rules apply as for the
Queen, the title used in the first instance being Your
Royal Highness, and subsequently Sir. Royal
princesses, whether married or unmarried, are called
in the first instance Your Royal Highness, and
subsequently Ma'am.

In writing   *Letter*

Sir (or Madam),

I have the honour to be, Sir (or Madam),
Your Royal Highness's most humble and obedient
servant,

In writing   *Envelope*

To His (or Her) Royal Highness the Prince (or
Princess) . . . .

or

To His (or Her) Royal Highness the Duke (or
Duchess) of . . . .

Camilla, Duchess of Cornwall

**In speech
and writing**
The same rules apply as for Duchesses
(page 13).

THE PEERAGE: General notes

The peerage has five descending, hereditary degrees. They are **Dukes, Marquesses, Earls, Viscounts** and **Barons**. We will begin with some general remarks applying to all degrees before taking the five degrees in turn. Rules for each separately appear in sections beginning on pages 13, 22, 31, 39 and 45.

Peers and the House of Lords Since the House of Lords Act 1999, few hereditary peers sit in the House of Lords. Today the majority of peers active in the House of Lords are the **Life Peers** (page 6), the **Lords Spiritual** (page 80) and the **Law Lords** (page 141) but the last-named are normally members of the legal profession on whom a peerage has been conferred.

Devolving titles

A hereditary title descends only in the oldest direct line, that is from father to son, or grandfather to grandson, except in such instances as will be mentioned, in which descent also includes the female line, and those in which remainder is expressly granted.

In the case of an ancient peerage, succession sometimes devolves upon a distant cousin, but he succeeds not because he is a cousin of the preceding peer, but because he is descended from some former holder of the title.

The brother or nephew of a newly created peer would not succeed to his honours unless special remainder were granted to his Patent, nor would a cousin of an older creation, unless his descent were from a former holder of it. This explains why some peers succeeding take lower titles than their predecessors. The 9th Earl of Drogheda, for instance, gained the title through descent from the fifth earl. The sixth earl was raised to the marquessate, which was held also by the seventh and eighth earls, as his direct descendants. But with the death of the third marquess the direct male descent from the first died out, though descent from previous holders of the lower title did not.

Courtesy titles

All peers have a family name as well as their titles, although in numerous cases, especially in the lower ranks of the peerage, the two are the same. The family name is used by the sons and daughters of peers, except in the cases of eldest sons of dukes, marquesses and earls.

In almost every case peers of these three categories have lesser titles also, of which the eldest son usually takes the highest as his courtesy title and uses it in every way as if it were his by right. In the few cases where there are no second titles, as in the earldoms of Devon, Huntingdon, and Temple of Stowe, the family name is used as a courtesy title. The eldest son of a duke is born in the degree of a marquess, but his courtesy title depends upon his father's lesser dignities. He takes the highest of these, which may be only that of an earl, a viscount, or a baron. He takes his title from birth, and, when he marries, his wife becomes a marchioness or a countess, or whatever it may be, and his children take the titles attached to those ranks. The eldest son of an eldest son takes a third title from the ducal collection, but of a lower grade than that of his father.

The correct ways of using these titles will be found under their various headings. They are in all respects the same, whether they are actual or courtesy titles, except that the prefixes, Most Honourable and Right Honourable, or The (which stands in their place; *see* page 8), are not used for courtesy titles.

Addressing the Heir on Succession

Until after his predecessor's funeral it is customary to continue to address the heir of a peerage or baronetcy by the courtesy title or other style by which he was formerly known.

Collaterals

All courtesy titles, or titles connected with the family name of a peer, are attached only to the actual descendants of that peer, with one occasional exception. It is that when a peer is succeeded by other than a son, the new peer's brothers and sisters may take the titles that would have been theirs if their father had succeeded.* In such cases he *would* have succeeded had he lived, so the honour really comes through him. His widow, however, if he has left one, does not share this privilege.

For instance, the 8th Duke of Devonshire died without issue. His heir was the eldest son of his brother, Lord Edward Cavendish, who had predeceased him. As long as the 8th duke lived his heir presumptive had no title, nor of course had his two brothers. But when Mr Victor Cavendish succeeded to the dukedom, his brothers became Lord Richard and Lord John Cavendish. His mother, however, remained Lady Edward Cavendish.

*These privileges cannot be claimed as a right. They are given by favour of the Crown, and warrants are granted in such cases only upon the recommendation of the Home Secretary.

Life Peers

Life peers rank with hereditary barons and baronesses according to the date of their creation. Wives of life peers take the title of Lady, and their children The Honourable. Husbands of women life peers do not take any title. Children of women life peers, however, take the title The Honourable. In all respects, except that the title does not descend, rules as for **Barons** and **Baronesses** apply (*see* page 45).

Territorial Additions

All peerages have still, as in their origin, a territorial basis, which is expressed in the Letters Patent creating a new peerage, as Baron Smith, of (a place with which the new Baron has connections) in the County of . . . . . This, which may be described as the 'address' of the peerage, does not form part of the title, and should never be used as though it did. There is, however, an increasing tendency to do so.

Some peerages, however, have a territorial addition included in their titles, to avoid confusion with older peerages of the same name (whether or not these still survive). In these cases, of which the Baronies of Morris, Morris of Borth-y-Gest, Morris of Grasmere, and Morris of Kenwood make a good example, the Letters Patent will read, e.g. Baron Morris of Grasmere, of Grasmere in the County of Westmorland, and it will be clear that the territorial addition forms part of the title, and should be used in addressing or referring to the peer. It is not possible for peers to change their titles from the form in which they were first created.

(*See also* page 65 for the Scottish use of territorial additions.)

New Peerages

When a new peerage is created, it is not possible to address the new peer as Lord or Lady . . . . immediately, because the title must be decided and the Letters Patent prepared. The new title will then be gazetted. If Hilary Smith receives a peerage, he or she retains the existing form of address until becoming, e.g. Baron(ess) Smith of Newtown; no title can be used until the actual title is known. (But *see* page 63 for new knighthoods, etc).

Disclaiming of Hereditary Peerages

The Peerage Act of 1963 authorised the disclaimer for life of certain hereditary peerages. A peer who disclaims his peerage loses all titles and precedence attached to it; he cannot, however, disclaim a baronetcy or a knighthood, and if he possesses one will be known by the appropriate title. His wife also loses the title and precedence which she received from her husband's hereditary peerage, although not, of course, any title and precedence she may herself have possessed. The eldest son of a disclaimed peer may continue if he wishes to use the courtesy title he used previously, and other children to use the titles Lord, Lady or The Honourable.

The Prefix 'The'

Members of the peerage are entitled by ancient custom, almost amounting to a right, to the following appellations:

Dukes – The Most Noble,
Marquesses – The Most Honourable,
Other Peers – The Right Honourable.

The practice is not to make use of the full title of peers when referring to them, but to shorten the prefix to 'The' as 'The Duke of Norfolk'.

The use of 'The Lord' is really short for 'The Most Hon. Lord' or 'The Right Hon. Lord'. When 'Lord' is used without a prefix it is for a courtesy title.

Where any peer is entitled to the additional prefix of Right Honourable by virtue of a Privy Counsellorship (*see* page 72), the addition merges in that attaching to the existing title; but Dukes and

Marquesses retain the right to both their designations in legal documents and formal circumstances. 'The Right Hon.' should not be shortened to 'The' (as above) when a peer is also a Privy Counsellor; his membership of the Privy Council entitles him to the full prefix at all times. Membership of the Privy Council being an office and not an honour, the initials PC should not be appended to any name or title (*and see* page 163).

The Title 'Lady'

This is probably the commonest of all, as it is used of all peeresses under the rank of duchess, of all daughters of the three highest ranks of the peerage, and of the wives of baronets and knights. Since 1958 it has also been used of life peers, baronesses by rank.

The prefix 'The' was once by general custom used in addressing the daughters of dukes, marquesses and earls, e.g. 'The Lady Jean Smith'. The practice existed only by courtesy, and was not recognised as correct by, for example, the College of Arms; it is no longer generally used, although it would be wrong to deprive elderly ladies of the prefix should they feel strongly about it.

Widows (including Dowagers when they so wish) or former wives use their forename before the title (See below and entries under Peerage, Baronetage and Knights.) They do not retain their husbands' titles on re-marriage.

The Title 'Honourable'

This title is a fairly frequent one, including as it does the younger sons of earls, all the sons and daughters of viscounts and barons, and the wives of the sons, beside its use outside the ranks of the peerage. The important rule to note is that it is *never* used in speech. Neither is it used in letter-writing, except on the envelope. (*See also* page 138 for uses outside the peerage.)

Peeresses in Their Own Right

Some baronies and a few earldoms descend in the female line. A peeress in her own right is addressed exactly as though the rank were obtained through marriage.

Husbands and Children of Peeresses in Their Own Right

Husbands take no style or dignity from their wives. Their children, however, are in all respects as if the peerage were held by their father.

Dowagers

These rules apply to the five grades of the peerage and also to the baronetage.

A dowager peeress is the earliest surviving widow of a preceding holder of the title, irrespective of her relationship to the existing holder. She may thus be mother, grandmother, aunt, great-aunt, etc.

Example The Dowager Duchess of Middlesex

Socially, however, a dowager peeress may prefer to be known not as Dowager, but by her forename; if this is so, she will probably make an announcement in the press of the style she prefers.

Where a Dowager is alive, succeeding widows use their forename.

Example Mary, Duchess of Middlesex

If the existing peer has no wife, the widow of his predecessor usually prefers to be addressed as if her husband were still alive, without prefix or Christian name.

When the Dowager dies, the next senior widow becomes the Dowager.

In Scotland the style of Dowager is applied only where the peeress is mother or grandmother of the present peer; it is carefully retained in Scottish families, since it emphasises that the widow became ancestress of an heir.

Former Wives of Peers

The wife of a peer whose marriage has been dissolved uses her forename.

Example Mary, Duchess of Middlesex

Peeresses Re-marrying

A peeress who re-marries loses the title she acquired by marriage to a peer; but retains or resumes any title she previously bore in her own right, or as the daughter of a peer.

Husbands and Children of Peers' Daughters

A husband's name or status is not altered in any way by his wife's degree. The children have no distinctions of any sort through their mother.

Peerage of Scotland

The Peerage of Scotland (that is, peerages created in Scotland before the Act of Union of 1707) has two distinctive features.

The lowest grade of the peerage is not Baron (which in Scots law denotes the property of a territorial estate held by Baronial charter), but Lord of Parliament. This should not be confused with the judicial title given to a Judge of the Court of Session in Scotland (*see* page 147). In practice the difference has little effect, since Barons are known and addressed as Lord in any case; but where it is

desired to show the exact title, it is, in the case of
Scottish lordships created before 1707, not Baron
Gray (for example), but Lord Gray. Scottish Lords
and Ladies and their families are addressed in all
ways the same as Barons and Baronesses (*see* page
45), with the exception which follows.

The second feature peculiar to Scottish peerages
is the title of Master given to the heir, whether
apparent or presumptive (also to the eldest son of an
heir who bears a courtesy title). The heir to a Duke,
a Marquess or an Earl who is entitled to use a
courtesy title will do so, rather than be known as
Master of . . . . ; but the heir to a Viscount or
Lord, and the eldest son of a Viscount or Lord by
courtesy, is known as Master. The title is nearly
always derived from that to which the bearer is heir;
thus Viscount Falkland's heir is the Master of
Falkland, and Lord Napier and Ettrick's the Master
of Napier. Their wives are called The Hon. Mrs . .
. . , without the husband's forename.

Example The Master of Ballantrae
The Hon. Mrs Scott of Ballantrae

In speech

Formerly styled 'My Lord', the Master is nowadays
called Sir on formal occasions, otherwise by his
surname, Mr Scott. In the household and family he
is referred to as The Master, and servants address
him as Master. His wife is called Mrs Scott.

In writing   *Letter*

Formally   Sir (or Dear Sir),
Madam,

Socially   Dear Mr Scott,
Dear Mrs Scott,

Envelope

The Master of Ballantrae
The Hon. Mrs Scott of Ballantrae

THE PEERAGE:
Dukes and Duchesses

The titles of all existing dukedoms are taken from the name of a place. (There are no instances of the title being taken from the family name. In those cases where the two are the same, the family name has been taken from the place.)

Example To help us in our explanation we will create a Duke of Middlesex, who is also Marquess of Huddersfield and Earl of Ramsgate, to name only his principal titles. His family shall be Smith.

The formal style of a Duke is 'The Most Noble the Duke of . . . . ', but the form of address for those of social equality is Duke of Middlesex or Duchess of Middlesex, the necessity for using the full title generally being avoided. For instance, if there is no need to distinguish between different dukes and duchesses, plain Duke or Duchess is correct. They are referred to as The Duke or The Duchess.

The archaic style of the title in conjunction with a forename, e.g. Duke John, is not now used. To distinguish a particular duke from others of his line he is called John, Duke of . . . . , or The Second Duke of . . . . .

In speech

In conversation it is best to make as sparing a use as possible of titles. Formally addressed as Your Grace, they are referred to as His Grace and Her Grace.

In writing

Letter

Formally

My Lord Duke,
I remain,
Your Grace's most obedient servant,

Madam,
I remain,
Your Grace's most obedient servant,

In writing	*Letter*
Less formally	My Lord Duke, Yours faithfully,
	Madam, Yours faithfully,
Socially	Dear Duke of Middlesex, Yours sincerely,
	or more familiarly
	Dear Duke, Yours sincerely,
	Dear Duchess of Middlesex, Yours sincerely,
	or more familiarly
	Dear Duchess, Yours sincerely,
	Envelope
Formally	His Grace the Duke of Middlesex Her Grace the Duchess of Middlesex
Socially	The prefix His Grace or Her Grace may be omitted, but The should then be retained.

Dowager Duchesses

A dowager duchess is so called when she is the earliest surviving widow of a preceding duke, irrespective of her relationship to the reigning duke (*but see* page 10 for Scottish practice).

Example The Dowager Duchess of Middlesex

Later surviving widows are distinguished by the use of their forename before the title (*see* page 10).

Example Mary, Duchess of Middlesex

But if the existing duke has no wife, the widow of his predecessor is addressed in all respects as if her husband were alive.

Example The Duchess of Middlesex

In speech

The rules for addressing in speech are in all ways the same as for the duke's wife, but if confusion were threatened she would be referred to as The Dowager Duchess.

In writing

Letter

Formally

Madam,

I remain,
Your Grace's most obedient servant,

or

Madam,
Yours faithfully,

Socially

Dear Duchess of Middlesex,
Yours sincerely,

or more familiarly

Dear Duchess,
Yours sincerely,

Envelope

Formally

Her Grace the Dowager Duchess of Middlesex *or* Her Grace Mary, Duchess of Middlesex

Socially

The prefix Her Grace may be omitted but The should then be retained.

Former Wives of Dukes

In speech

They are addressed as Madam or Duchess; referred to as Mary, Duchess of Middlesex.

In writing	*Letter*
Formally	Madam,
	I remain, Madam,
	Your most obedient servant,
	or
	Madam,
	Yours faithfully,
Socially	Dear Duchess of Middlesex,
	Yours sincerely,
	or more familiarly
	Dear Duchess,
	Yours sincerely,

Envelope

Mary, Duchess of Middlesex

Eldest Sons of Dukes

(*See also* under **Courtesy Titles**, page 5)

The eldest son of a duke is born in the degree of a marquess, but his courtesy title depends upon his father's lesser dignities. He normally takes the highest of these, which may be only that of an earl or lesser degree. He takes his title from birth, and, when he marries, his wife and children share the honours attached to his rank.

Example The eldest son of our Duke of Middlesex would be Marquess of Huddersfield and his wife Marchioness of Hudderfield. Their eldest son would be Earl of Ramsgate.

The correct use of these titles will be found under their various headings. It is in all respects the same, whether they are actual or courtesy titles, except that the prefix Most Honourable, or 'The', which represents it, is not used, i.e. Marquess of Huddersfield, not The Most Honourable the Marquess of Huddersfield. (*See* page 8.)

Widows of Eldest Sons of Dukes
Former Wives of Eldest Sons of Dukes

Rules will vary according to the title of the Eldest Son.

Children of Eldest Sons of Dukes

The eldest son takes a third title from the ducal collection, of a lower grade than that of his father. Titles of his brothers and sisters will depend on the father's title.

Daughters and Younger Sons of Dukes

The younger sons of a duke bear the title 'Lord' with their Christian and family names, and all daughters of a duke bear the title 'Lady'.

Examples Lord John Smith
Lady Barbara Smith

In this category the commonest mistakes are made by those who do not know the distinctions between the sorts of people who are entitled to be called 'Lord' or 'Lady'. Lord John Smith must *never* be called Lord Smith, nor Lady Barbara Smith Lady Smith.

In speech

When the full titles are not used they are called Lord John and Lady Barbara. There is no other abbreviation unless one is on such terms of intimacy as to use their forenames alone.

In writing

Letter

Formally

My Lord,

I have the honour to remain,
Your Lordship's obedient servant,

My Lady (or Madam),

I have the honour to remain,
Your Ladyship's obedient servant,

In writing	*Letter*
Less formally	My Lord, Yours faithfully,
	Madam, Yours faithfully,
Socially	Dear Lord John Smith, Yours sincerely,
	or more familiarly
	Dear Lord John, Yours sincerely,
Socially	Dear Lady Barbara Smith, Yours sincerely,
	or more familiarly
	Dear Lady Barbara, Yours sincerely,

Envelope

Lord John Smith

Lady Barbara Smith

Wives of Younger Sons of Dukes

The mistake already alluded to in this category is made most often in the case of wives of younger sons of dukes and marquesses. The wife of Lord John Smith is Lady John Smith, and never in any circumstances Lady Smith. She is known less formally as Lady John. This rule is varied only when she is of higher rank than her husband, in which case her own forename is substituted for his (*See* under **Married Daughters of Dukes**, page 20.)

In speech	Lady John Smith
	or, more familiarly
	Lady John

In writing	*Letter*
Formally	Madam (or My Lady), I have the honour to remain, Your Ladyship's obedient servant,
Less formally	Madam, Yours faithfully,
Socially	Dear Lady John Smith, Yours sincerely,
	or, more familiarly
	Dear Lady John, Yours sincerely,

Envelope

Lady John Smith

Widows of Younger Sons of Dukes

If the widow of a younger son of a duke, having no title of her own, re-marries, she may not continue to use her late husband's name and title. If, on the other hand, she has a title of her own, she will use it coupled with her new name. If she re-marries into the peerage, she will obviously share her second husband's name and title.

Former Wives of Younger Sons of Dukes

The same rules apply to former wives as to widows.

Children of Younger Sons of Dukes

The children of younger sons of dukes have no distinctions of any sort. All the sons and daughters of Lord and Lady John Smith would be plain Mr or Miss. A popular fallacy would make them honourables, but that is quite wrong. They have, of course, some precedence in the social scale.

Married Daughters of Dukes

The daughter of a duke, in marrying a peer (not a courtesy peer), shares her husband's title and precedence.

In all other cases she retains her own title of Lady with her forename even if she marries the younger son of a duke, because by a curious anomaly all peers' daughters rank one degree higher than younger sons of the same grade. In the event of marriage with the heir of an earl or lesser peer, she is entitled, if she prefers it, to retain her own title while her husband is a courtesy lord, because she actually keeps her precedence until he succeeds to his peerage. There are instances of both usages in the peerage, and the chosen style should be ascertained in each case.

Marriage with a commoner does not alter her rank in any way (nor, incidentally, that of her husband). Our duke's daughter, Lady Barbara Smith, married to Mr Peter Green, would become Lady Barbara Green. In no circumstances would she be called Lady Peter Green. Together they would be referred to as Mr Peter and Lady Barbara Green, or Mr and Lady Barbara Green.

Curiously enough, however, the daughter of a duke (as also of a marquess or earl) keeps her rank as such in the table of precedence if she marries out of the peerage, but exchanges it for that of her husband if she remains in it, even if it means descending several steps. Thus Lady Barbara having married Mr Peter Green, would go in to dinner before a sister who had married a baron.

Examples Marriage with

a commoner	Peter Green, Esq.	Lady Barbara Green
Scottish chief or laird	James MacBrown of Glenbrown	Lady Barbara MacBrown of Glenbrown
a knight or baronet	Sir Bernard Brown	Lady Barbara Brown
a younger son of an earl or lesser peer	The Honourable George Wilson	Lady Barbara Wilson
an eldest son of an earl	Viscount Staines (Lord Staines)	Lady Barbara Staines, *or* Viscountess Staines (Lady Staines), as she prefers
a younger son of a duke or marquess	Lord John Bull	Lady Barbara Bull
an eldest son of a marquess	Earl of Malvern (Lord Malvern)	Countess of Malvern (Lady Malvern) *or* Lady Barbara Malvern, as she prefers
an eldest son of a duke	Marquess of Mere (Lord Mere)	Marchioness of Mere (Lady Mere)
a peer of any rank	The Right Hon. Lord Slough (The Lord Slough)	The Right Hon. Lady Slough (The Lady Slough)

Children of Daughters of Dukes

The children of daughters of dukes receive no titles or distinctions of any sort through their mother.

THE PEERAGE:
Marquesses and Marchionesses

This title is rendered in two ways, marquess or
marquis. The former is the older and purely British.
Peers of this rank use which form they prefer, and
their choice should be ascertained and observed in
addressing them.

Territorial/non-Territorial Titles
The title of marquess is generally taken from the
name of a place, as it invariably is in the case of a
duke.

Example The Marquess of Montgomeryshire

There are two marquessates in our peerage, however,
whose titles are taken from the family names, and in
both these cases the preposition is dropped, thus:

The Marquess Conyngham
The Marquess Townshend

In two other cases there is no preposition even
though the titles are territorial, viz.,

The Marquess Camden
The Marquess Douro (the present Marquess
prefers to be addressed as the Marquess of Douro)

Example Our typical peer of this, the second grade,
shall be the Marquess of Montgomeryshire, who is
also the Earl of Malvern and Baron Swindon. His
family name shall be Evans.

In speech

It has been said already that all peers and peeresses
below ducal rank are called Lord and Lady in
speech. This brings us to a mistake quite commonly
made in connection with the lower grades of the
peerage. Although it is correct to talk of the Duke,
or Duchess of Middlesex – indeed, they could not be
referred to in any other way – the rule is quite
different for the marquessate. The Marquess and
Marchioness of Montgomeryshire would always be

addressed as My Lord and My Lady, and referred to as Lord and Lady Montgomeryshire. There are a few formal occasions on which the full title would be used, but it would never occur in intimate speech.

In writing	*Letter*
Formally	My Lord Marquess, *or* My Lord, I have the honour to be, Your Lordship's obedient servant, Madam, I have the honour to remain, Your Ladyship's obedient servant,
Less formally	My Lord, Yours faithfully, Madam, Yours faithfully,
Socially	Dear Lord Montgomeryshire, *or* Dear Montgomeryshire, Yours sincerely, Dear Lady Montgomeryshire, Yours sincerely,
	Envelope
Formally	The Most Hon. the Marquess of Montgomeryshire The Most Hon. the Marchioness of Montgomeryshire
Socially	The Marquess of Montgomeryshire The Marchioness of Montgomeryshire

Dowager Marchionesses

A dowager marchioness is so called when she is the earliest surviving widow of a preceding marquess, irrespective of her relationship to the present marquess (*but see* page 10 for Scottish practice). A later surviving widow is distinguished by the use of her forename before her title (*see* page 10).

Examples The Dowager Marchioness of
Montgomeryshire
Enid, Marchioness of Montgomeryshire

In speech

Both would be addressed as Madam and referred to as Lady Montgomeryshire.

In writing

Letter

Formally

Madam,

I have the honour to remain,
Your Ladyship's obedient servant,

Less formally

Madam,
Yours faithfully,

Socially

Dear Lady Montgomeryshire,
Yours sincerely,

Envelope

Formally

The Most Hon. the Dowager Marchioness of
Montgomeryshire *or*
The Most Hon. Enid, Marchioness of
Montgomeryshire

Socially

The Dowager Marchioness of Montgomeryshire *or*
Enid, Marchioness of Montgomeryshire

Former Wives of Marquesses

The former wife of a Marquess uses her forename before the title unless she re-marries.

In speech

She is addressed as Madam and referred to as Lady Montgomeryshire.

In writing

Letter

Formally

Madam,

I have the honour to remain,
Your Ladyship's obedient servant,

Less formally	Madam,
	Yours faithfully,
Socially	Dear Lady Montgomeryshire,
	Yours sincerely,

Envelope

| Formally | Enid, Marchioness of Montgomeryshire |
| Socially | Enid, Marchioness of Montgomeryshire |

Eldest Sons of Marquesses

(*See also under* **Courtesy Titles**, page 5)

As stated elsewhere, peers in this category have lesser titles as well, and the eldest son usually takes the highest of these as his courtesy title, which is used in every way as if it were his by right. He takes the title from birth, and on his marriage his wife and children share the honours attached to his rank. His eldest son would take a third title from among the marquess's lesser titles.

Example The eldest son of our Marquess of Montgomeryshire would be Earl of Malvern and his wife Countess of Malvern. Their eldest son would be Baron Swindon. The correct use of these titles will be found under their various headings. It is in all respects the same, whether they are actual or courtesy titles, except that the prefix Right Honourable, or 'The', which represents it, is not used, e.g. Earl of Malvern (*see* page 8).

Widows of Eldest Sons of Marquesses
Former Wives of Eldest Sons of Marquesses
Children of Eldest Sons of Marquesses

Rules will vary according to the title of the Eldest Son.

Younger Sons of Marquesses

The younger sons of a marquess bear the title Lord and their forename and family name.

Example Lord Charles Evans

Lord Charles Evans must *never* be called Lord Evans.

In speech   When the full title is not used, he is called Lord Charles. There is no other abbreviation.

In writing   *Letter*

Formally   My Lord,
I have the honour to remain,
Your Lordship's obedient servant,

Less formally   My Lord,
Yours faithfully,

Socially   Dear Lord Charles Evans,
Yours sincerely,

or more familiarly

Dear Lord Charles,
Yours sincerely,

Envelope
Lord Charles Evans

Wives of Younger Sons of Marquesses

The mistake already alluded to in this category is made most often in the case of wives of younger sons of dukes and marquesses. The wife of Lord Charles Evans is Lady Charles Evans, and *never* in any circumstances Lady Evans. This rule is varied only when she is of higher rank than her husband, in which case her own forename is substituted for his. (*See under* **Married Daughters of Marquesses**, page 28.)

In speech	She is known less formally as Lady Charles.
In writing	*Letter*
Formally	Madam (or My Lady), I have the honour to remain, Your Ladyship's obedient servant,
Less formally	Madam, Yours faithfully,
Socially	Dear Lady Charles Evans, Yours sincerely, *or more familiarly* Dear Lady Charles, Yours sincerely, *Envelope* Lady Charles Evans

Widows and Former Wives of Younger Sons of Marquesses

If the widow of a younger son of a marquess, having no title of her own, re-marries, she may not continue to use her late husband's name and title. If, on the other hand, she has a title of her own, she will use it coupled with her new name. The same rules apply to former wives as to widows.

Children of Younger Sons of Marquesses

The children of younger sons of marquesses have no distinctions of any sort. All the sons and daughters of Lord and Lady Charles Evans would be plain Mr and Miss. They have, of course, some precedence in the social scale.

Daughters of Marquesses

All daughters of a marquess bear the title Lady with their forename and family name.

Example Lady Joan Evans

Lady Joan Evans must *never* be called Lady Evans.

In speech

When the full title is not used, she is called Lady Joan. There is no other abbreviation.

In writing

Letter

Formally

Madam (or My Lady),
I have the honour to remain,
Your Ladyship's obedient servant,

Less formally

Madam,
Yours faithfully,

Socially

Dear Lady Joan Evans,
Yours sincerely,

or more familiarly

Dear Lady Joan,
Yours sincerely,

Envelope

Lady Joan Evans

Married Daughters of Marquesses

The daughter of a marquess, in marrying a peer (not a courtesy peer), shares her husband's title and precedence, as also if she marries a man of equal or higher rank than her own – the eldest son of a marquess or any son of a duke. In all other cases she retains her own title of Lady with her forename, even if she marries the younger son of a marquess, because, as stated elsewhere, all peers' daughters rank one degree higher than younger sons of the same grade. In the event of marriage with the heir of an earl or lesser peer, she is entitled, if she prefers it, to retain her own title while her husband is a courtesy lord, because she actually keeps her precedence until he succeeds to his peerage. There are instances of both usages in the peerage, and the chosen style should be ascertained in each case.

Marriage with a commoner does not alter her rank in any way (nor, incidentally, that of her husband). Our marquess's daughter, married to Mr Peter Green, would become Lady Joan Green. In no circumstances would she be called Lady Peter Green. Together they would be described as Mr Peter and Lady Joan Green.

Curiously enough, however, the daughter of a marquess (as also of a duke or earl) keeps her rank as such in the table of precedence if she marries out of the peerage, but exchanges it for that of her husband if she remains in it, even if it means descending several steps. Thus Lady Joan, having married Mr Peter Green, would go in to dinner before a sister who had married a baron.

Examples Marriage with

a commoner	Peter Green, Esq	Lady Joan Green
a knight or baronet	Sir Bernard Brown	Lady Joan Brown
a younger son of an earl or letter peer	The Honourable George Wilson	Lady Joan Wilson
an eldest son of an earl	Viscount Staines (Lord Staines)	Lady Joan Staines *or* Viscountess Staines (Lady Staines), as she prefers
a younger son of a marquess	Lord John Bull	Lady Joan Bull
a younger son of a duke	Lord John Smith	Lady John Smith, *or* Lady Joan Smith, as she prefers
an eldest son of a marquess	Earl of Malvern (Lord Malvern)	Countess of Malvern (Lady Malvern)
an eldest son of a duke	Marquess of Mere (Lord Mere)	Marchioness of Mere (Lady Mere)
a peer of any rank	The Right Hon. Lord Slough (The Lord Slough)	The Right Hon. Lady Slough (The Lady Slough)

Children of Daughters of Marquesses

The children of daughters of marquesses receive no titles or distinctions of any sort through their mother.

THE PEERAGE:
Earls and Countesses

This grade is sometimes territorial, sometimes taken from the family name. In the former case the preposition 'of' is generally used, and in the latter case it is not, although there are numerous exceptions to both rules.

In one or two instances, such as the Earl of Winchilsea and Nottingham, two separate earldoms have become merged. Both titles are used on all formal occasions and even on the social envelope. But in social speech and letters only the first one is employed.

The Earl of Winchilsea and Nottingham's title provides an instance of the little traps which are sometimes, almost perversely it would seem, set for the unwary. The name of the ancient town from which Lord Winchilsea takes his title is spelt Winchelsea. Another curious instance is that the town of Beaconsfield, from which Disraeli took his title, is pronounced Beckonsfield. He lived within a few miles of it at Hughenden, and must have been aware of this. But his title was pronounced by him as it is written, and continues to be so pronounced.

Example Our typical peer in this, the third grade, shall be the Earl of Whitby, with a second title, Viscount Staines, and the family name of Collins.

In speech

It has been remarked already that all peers and peeresses below ducal rank are called lord and lady in speech. This rule applies, of course, to earls and countesses, who are always referred and spoken to as lord and lady. As in the case of the marquessate, there are a few formal occasions on which the full title would be used, but it would never happen in intimate speech.

In writing	*Letter*
Formally	My Lord,
	I have the honour to remain,
	Your Lordship's obedient servant,
	Madam,
	I have the honour to remain,
	Your Ladyship's obedient servant,
Less formally	My Lord,
	Yours faithfully,
	Madam,
	Yours faithfully,
Socially	Dear Lord Whitby, *or*
	Dear Whitby,
	Yours sincerely,
	Dear Lady Whitby,
	Yours sincerely,
	Envelope
Formally	The Right Hon. the Earl of Whitby
	The Right Hon. the Countess of Whitby
Socially	The Earl of Whitby
	The Countess of Whitby

Dowager Countesses

A dowager countess is so called when she is the earliest surviving widow of a preceding earl (but *see* page 10 for Scottish practice). A later surviving widow is distinguished by the use of the forename before her title (*see* page 10).

Examples The Dowager Countess of Whitby
Muriel, Countess of Whitby

In speech Style is exactly the same as if she were the present countess.

In writing	*Letter*
Formally	Madam,
	I have the honour to remain,
	Your Ladyship's obedient servant,
Less formally	Madam,
	Yours faithfully,
Socially	Dear Lady Whitby,
	Yours sincerely,
	Envelope
Formally	The Right Hon. the Dowager Countess of Whitby
	or
	The Right Hon. Muriel, Countess of Whitby
Socially	The Dowager Countess of Whitby *or*
	Muriel, Countess of Whitby

Former Wives of Earls

The former wife of an Earl uses her forename before the title.

In writing	*Letter*
Formally	Madam,
	I have the honour to remain,
	Your Ladyship's obedient servant,
Less formally	Madam,
	Yours faithfully,
Socially	Dear Lady Whitby,
	Yours sincerely,
	Envelope
	Muriel, Countess of Whitby

Eldest Sons of Earls

(*See also* under **Courtesy Titles**, page 5).

As stated elsewhere, peers in this category have lesser titles as well, and the eldest son usually takes the highest of these as his courtesy title, which is used in every way as if it were his by right. He takes the title from birth, and on his marriage his wife and children share the honours attached to his rank.

Example The eldest son of our Earl of Whitby would be Viscount Staines and his wife Viscountess Staines. The correct use of these titles will be found under their various headings. It is in all respects the same whether they are actual or courtesy titles, with the exception that the prefix Right Honourable, or 'The', which represents it, is not used, e.g. Viscount Staines. (*See* page 8.)

Widows of Eldest Sons of Earls
Former Wives of Eldest Sons of Earls
Children of Eldest Sons of Earls

Rules will vary according to the title of the Eldest Son.

Younger Sons of Earls

Unlike the higher grades of the peerage, younger sons of earls are styled Honourable with their forenames and family names (not initials), and there is nothing to distinguish them from the sons of viscounts and barons.

Example The Honourable Thomas Collins

As remarked elsewhere, this title is never used in speech or letter-writing, except on the envelope.

The younger sons of earls are called Mr, always in conjunction with the forename.

Example Mr Thomas Collins

In speech

The title is never printed on visiting cards, so that without inner knowledge it is difficult to recognise the rank. When it is desired to indicate it, however, a reference to the holder's parentage would be permissible. Servants would announce the younger son of an earl as Mr Thomas Collins.

In writing

Letter

Formally

Sir,
I have the honour to be,
Your obedient servant,

Less formally

Dear Sir,
Yours faithfully,

Socially

Dear Mr Collins,
Yours sincerely,

Envelope

The Hon. Thomas Collins

Wives of Younger Sons of Earls

Wives of younger sons of earls share their husbands' title.

Example The Hon. Mrs Thomas Collins

It should be carefully noted that whereas it is wrong to use the designations Mr or Miss with this title, it is right to use the designation Mrs with it.

In speech

The title is never used in speech and the wife of Mr Thomas Collins is always alluded to as Mrs Thomas Collins. If she happens to be of higher rank than her husband, she would use her own title in conjunction with her husband's name – without the Honourable.

In writing	*Letter*
Formally	Madam,
	I have the honour to remain,
	Your obedient servant,
Less formally	Dear Madam,
	Yours faithfully
Socially	Dear Mrs Collins,
	Yours sincerely,

Envelope

The Hon. Mrs Thomas Collins

Widows of Younger Sons of Earls

Widows of younger sons of earls keep their title until re-marriage, when it is abandoned in favour of the second husband's status, whether it be higher or lower. If the widow possesses a title in her own right she will of course continue to use it.

Former Wives of Younger Sons of Earls

The same rules apply to former wives as to widows.

Children of Younger Sons of Earls

Children of younger sons of earls have no distinction of any sort. They have, of course, a certain social precedence.

Daughters of Earls

Daughters of earls bear the title Lady with their Christian and family names.

Example Lady Violet Collins

In speech	The same rules apply as in the case of daughters of dukes and marquesses, viz. when the full title is not used, our earl's daughter will be called Lady Violet. There is no other abbreviation unless one is on such terms of intimacy as to use the forename alone.

In writing

Letter

Formally

Madam (or My Lady),
I have the honour to remain,
Your Ladyship's obedient servant,

Less formally

Madam,
Yours faithfully,

Socially

Dear Lady Violet Collins,
Yours sincerely,

or more familiarly

Dear Lady Violet,
Yours sincerely,

Envelope
Lady Violet Collins

Married Daughters of Earls

The daughter of an earl, if she marries a peer (not a courtesy peer), or a man of equal or higher rank than her own, shares her husband's title and precedence. otherwise she retains her own title of Lady and her forename, even if she marries the younger son of an earl, because, as stated elsewhere, all peers' daughters rank one degree higher than younger sons of the same grade. In the event of marriage with the heir of a viscount or lesser peer, she is entitled, if she prefers it, to retain her own title until her husband succeeds to his peerage, because she actually keeps her own precedence until then. In such a case the chosen style should be ascertained.

Marriage with a commoner does not alter her rank in any way — nor, incidentally, that of her husband. Our earl's daughter, married to Mr Peter Green, would become Lady Violet Green. She must never be called Lady Peter Green. Together they would be described as Mr Peter and Lady Violet Green.

Curiously enough, however, the daughter of an earl keeps her rank as such in the table of precedence if she marries out of the peerage, but exchanges it for that of her husband if she remains in it, even if it means descending several steps. Thus Lady Violet, having married Mr Peter Green, would go in to dinner before a sister who had married a baron.

Examples Marriage with

a commoner	Mr Peter Green	Lady Violet Green
a knight or baronet	Sir Bernard Brown	Lady Violet Brown
a younger son of an earl or lesser peer	The Honourable Michael O'Mara	Lady Violet O'Mara
an eldest son of an earl	Viscount Staines (Lord Staines)	Viscountess Staines (Lady Staines)
a younger son of a marquess	Lord John Bull	Lady John Bull
a younger son of a duke	Lord John Smith	Lady John Smith
an eldest son of a marquess	Earl of Malvern (Lord Malvern)	Countess of Malvern (Lady Malvern)
an eldest son of a duke	Marquess of Mere (Lord Mere)	Marchioness of Mere (Lady Mere)
a peer of any rank	The Right Hon. Lord Slough (The Lord Slough)	The Right Hon. Lady Slough (The Lady Slough)

Children of Daughters of Earls

The children of daughters of earls receive no titles or distinctions of any sort through their mother.

THE PEERAGE:
Viscounts and Viscountesses

This title is sometimes territorial, sometimes derived from the family name, but in neither case is the preposition 'of' used between the style and the title, e.g. Viscount Hereford, not The Viscount of Hereford. Viscounts in the peerage of Scotland (or before 1707) *do* include the 'of', e.g. The Viscount of Arbuthnott. A number of viscounts recently created also contain a territorial addition to the title, e.g. Viscount Grey of Fallodon. In such cases the full style is used on formal occasions and in addressing all letters, formal and social.

Example Our example in this, the fourth grade of the peerage, shall be Viscount O'Mara, with the same family name.

In speech

The rule already explained, that all peers and peeresses below ducal rank are called lord and lady in speech, applies equally, of course, to viscounts and their wives. As in other ranks, there are a few formal occasions on which the full title would be used, but it would never happen in intimate speech.

In writing   *Letter*

Formally

My Lord,
I have the honour to remain,
Your Lordship's obedient servant,

Madam,
I have the honour to remain,
Your Ladyship's obedient servant,

Less formally

My Lord,
Yours faithfully,

Madam,
Yours faithfully,

In writing	*Letter*
Socially	Dear Lord O'Mara, *or* Dear O'Mara, Yours sincerely,
	Dear Lady O'Mara, Yours sincerely,
	Envelope
Formally	The Right Hon. the Viscount O'Mara The Right Hon. the Viscountess O'Mara
Socially	The Viscount O'Mara The Viscountess O'Mara

Dowager Viscountesses

A dowager viscountess is the earliest surviving widow of a preceding peer (*but see* page 10 for the Scottish practice). Later surviving widows are distinguished by the use of the forename before the title (*see* page 10).

In speech	Style is exactly the same as if she were the present viscountess (*see above*).
In writing	*Letter*
Formally	Madam,
	I have the honour to remain, Your Ladyship's obedient servant,
Less formally	Madam, Yours faithfully,
Socially	Dear Lady O'Mara, Yours sincerely,
	Envelope
Formally	The Right Hon. the Dowager Viscountess O'Mara *or* The Right Hon. Anne, Viscountess O'Mara

| Socially | The Dowager Viscountess O'Mara *or*
Anne, Viscountess O'Mara |

Former Wives of Viscounts

The former wife of a Viscount uses her forename before the title.

In speech   She will be addressed as My Lady.

In writing   *Letter*

Formally
> Madam,
> I have the honour to remain,
> Your Ladyship's obedient servant,

Less formally
> Madam,
> Yours faithfully,

Socially
> Dear Lady O'Mara,
> Yours sincerely,

Envelope

Anne, Viscountess O'Mara

Eldest Sons of Viscounts

Courtesy titles cease at the grade of an earl, so that the eldest son of a viscount does not take his father's second title, even if he happens to have one. Like his younger brothers, he is merely The Honourable, using his forename (not initials) and surname, and his wife shares the title.

Example The Hon. Michael O'Mara
             The Hon. Mrs Michael O'Mara

Their visiting cards would be inscribed 'Mr O'Mara' and 'Mrs O'Mara' without the forename.

In speech   As explained before, the title Honourable is never used in speech, so that the eldest son of our viscount would be spoken and referred to as Mr O'Mara and his wife as Mrs O'Mara.

In writing	*Letter*
Formally	Sir, I have the honour to remain, Your obedient servant, Madam, I have the honour to remain, Your obedient servant,
Less formally	Dear Sir, Yours faithfully, Dear Madam, Yours faithfully,
Socially	Dear Mr O'Mara, Yours sincerely, Dear Mrs O'Mara, Yours sincerely,

Envelope

The Hon. Michael O'Mara

The Hon. Mrs Michael O'Mara

Widows of Eldest Sons of Viscounts

Widows of eldest sons of viscounts keep their title until re-marriage, when it is abandoned in favour of the second husband's status, whether it be higher or lower. This does not apply, of course, if the widow possesses a title in her own right.

Former Wives of Eldest Sons of Viscounts

The same rules as above apply to former wives as to widows.

Children of Eldest Sons of Viscounts

Children of eldest sons of viscounts have no titles or distinctions of any sort. (*See* **Peerage of Scotland**, page 12).

Younger Sons of Viscounts
Wives of Younger Sons of Viscounts
Widows of Younger Sons of Viscounts
Former Wives of Younger Sons of Viscounts

Exactly the same rules apply here as to younger sons of earls and their wives (*see* pages 34 and 35).

Children of Younger Sons of Viscounts

Children of younger sons of viscounts have no titles or distinctions of any sort.

Daughters of Viscounts

Daughters of viscounts all bear the title Honourable, like their brothers.

In speech   The title is never used in speech. The eldest daughter is referred to as Miss O'Mara, the younger ones as, e.g. Miss Nora and Miss Bridget O'Mara.

In writing   *Letter*
Style is the same for all.

Formally   Madam,
I have the honour to remain,
Your obedient servant,

Less formally   Dear Madam,
Yours faithfully,

Socially   Dear Miss O'Mara,
Yours sincerely,

In writing

Envelope

The Hon. Eileen O'Mara

Married Daughters of Viscounts

The daughter of a viscount, in marrying a man of lower rank than her own, keeps her title, thus:

Marriage with

| a commoner | Mr Peter Green | The Hon. Mrs Green (not The Hon. Mrs Peter Green) |
| a knight or baronet | Sir Bernard Brown | The Hon. Lady Brown |

In marrying a man of equal or higher rank she shares her husband's title.

Children of Daughters of Viscounts

Children of daughters of viscounts have no titles or distinctions of any sort. They have, of course, a certain social precedence.

THE PEERAGE:
Barons and Baronesses

This is the fifth and last grade of the peerage. In England and Wales 'Baron' and 'Baroness' have always been the legal terms, whereas in Scotland the legal term for a hereditary peer of this rank whose title was created before 1707 is 'Lord' or 'Lady' (*see* **Peerage of Scotland**, page 11). In usage, however, all of this rank are known as 'Lord' or 'Lady', with the exception of peeresses in their own right (including women life peers) who may choose to be called 'Baroness'.

The title is sometimes territorial, sometimes taken from the family name, and sometimes from other sources entirely.

Example Our example shall be Baron Westley, family name Whitworth.

In speech

The rule of addressing all peers below ducal rank as lord and lady is equally applicable to barons and their wives. Baronesses in their own right, however (including women life peers), are called The Baroness . . . . if they so wish.

In writing

Letter

Formally

My Lord,
I have the honour to be,
Your Lordship's obedient servant,

Madam,
I have the honour to be,
Your Ladyship's obedient servant,

Less formally

My Lord,
Yours faithfully,

Madam,
Yours faithfully,

In writing	*Letter*
Socially	Dear Lord Westley, *or* Dear Westley, Yours sincerely, Dear Lady Westley, Yours sincerely,
	Envelope
Formally	The Right Hon. Lord Westley The Right Hon. Lady Westley
Socially	The Lord Westley The Lady Westley

Dowager Baronesses

A dowager baroness is the earliest surviving widow of a preceding peer (*but see* page 10 for the Scottish practice). Later surviving widows are distinguished by the use of the forename before the title (*see* page 10).

In speech	Style is exactly the same as if she were the present baroness (*see above*).
In writing	*Letter*
Formally	Madam, I have the honour to remain, Your Ladyship's obedient servant,
Less formally	Madam, Yours faithfully,
Socially	Dear Lady Westley, Yours sincerely,
	Envelope
Formally	The Right Hon. the Dowager Lady Westley *or* The Right Hon. Anne, Lady Westley
Socially	The Dowager Lady Westley, *or* Anne, Lady Westley

Former Wives of Barons

The former wife of a baron uses her forename before the title.

In speech

She will be addressed as My Lady.

In writing

Letter

Formally

Madam,
I have the honour to remain,
Your Ladyship's obedient servant,

Less formally

Madam,
Yours faithfully,

Socially

Dear Lady Westley,
Yours sincerely,

Envelope

Anne, Lady Westley

Eldest Sons of Barons

Courtesy titles cease at the grade of an earl, so that the eldest son of a baron, like his younger brothers, is merely The Honourable, and his wife shares the title. 'The Honourable' is followed by a forename rather than initials.

Example The Hon. Roger Whitworth
The Hon. Mrs Roger Whitworth

Their visiting cards would be inscribed Mr Whitworth and Mrs Whitworth, without the forename.

In speech

As explained elsewhere, the title Honourable is never used in speech, so that the eldest son of our baron would be spoken and referred to as Mr Whitworth and his wife as Mrs Whitworth.

In writing	*Letter*
Formally	Sir,
	I have the honour to remain,
	Your obedient servant,
	Madam,
	I have the honour to remain,
	Your obedient servant,
Less formally	Dear Sir,
	Yours faithfully,
	Dear Madam,
	Yours faithfully,
Socially	Dear Mr Whitworth,
	Yours sincerely
	Dear Mrs Whitworth,
	Yours sincerely,

Envelope

The Hon. Roger Whitworth

The Hon. Mrs Roger Whitworth

Widows of Eldest Sons of Barons
Former Wives of Eldest Sons

Widows and former wives of eldest sons of barons keep their title until re-marriage, when it is abandoned in favour of the second husband's status, whether it be higher or lower. This does not apply, of course, if the widow or former wife possesses a title in her own right.

Children of Eldest Sons of Barons

Children of eldest sons of barons have no titles or distinctions of any sort. (*See* **Peerage of Scotland**, page 12.)

Younger Sons of Barons
Wives of Younger Sons of Barons
Widows of Younger Sons of Barons
Former Wives of Younger Sons of Barons

Exactly the same rules apply here as to younger sons of earls and their wives *(see* pages 34 and 35).

Children of Younger Sons of Barons

Children of younger sons of barons have no titles or distinctions of any sort.

Daughters of Barons

All bear the title of Honourable, and the same rules apply as for daughters of viscounts *(see* page 43).

Married Daughters of Barons

The daughter of a baron, in marrying a man of lower rank than her own, keeps her title, thus:

Marriage with

a commoner	Mr Peter Green	The Hon. Mrs Green (not The Hon. Mrs Peter Green)
a knight or baronet	Sir Bernard Brown	The Hon. Lady Brown

In marrying a man of equal or higher rank she shares her husband's title.

Children of Daughters of Barons

Children of daughters of barons have no titles or distinctions of any sort.

THE BARONETAGE

The title of baronet, identified by the prefix Sir to Christian and surname, is a hereditary honour descending from father to son. Failing a son to the first holder, the title becomes extinct; but failing a son to a later holder, the title goes to the nearest male descendant of a former holder. It is distinguished from that of knight by the word baronet, or one of its contractions, being added at the end of the name.

Example Sir George Robinson, Bt

Where a Scottish family uses a territorial title this is inserted before the addition 'Bt'.

Example Sir George Robinson of Glenrobinson, Bt

The word baronet is used in full only in formal documents. Bt is the older abbreviation and the only one recognised by the Council of the Baronetage, but, in spite of this, Bart is still much used. This is a pity, because it is considered wrong by those who know and prefer the right way.

A baronet's wife takes the title of Lady in conjunction with the surname only – never with her own or her husband's forename unless she happens to have a title of her own (*see* pages 9, 21, 29, 38, 44 and 49).

Example Lady Robinson

The only exception to this rule might be the written one of Lady (George) Robinson, when it is necessary to distinguish her from another Lady Robinson. In actual speech there can be no such distinction. In Scotland, however, the territorial addition (if it exists) acts as the distinction.

Example Lady Robinson of Glenrobinson.

Lady Robinson is not entitled to be called The Lady Robinson (*see* page 9).

In speech	A baronet is addressed by his title and forename, as, for instance, Sir George, and spoken of as Sir George Robinson, or, more familiarly, as Sir George. There is no distinction here between a baronet and a knight.
In writing	*Letter*
Formally	Sir, I have the honour to remain, Your obedient servant, Madam, I have the honour to remain, Your Ladyship's obedient servant,
Less formally	Dear Sir, Yours faithfully, Dear Madam, Yours faithfully,
Socially	Dear Sir George Robinson, Yours faithfully, *or more familiarly* Dear Sir George, Yours sincerely, Dear Lady Robinson, Yours sincerely,
	Envelope
Formally	Sir George Robinson, Bt Sir George Robinson of Glenrobinson, Bt Lady Robinson Lady Robinson of Glenrobinson
Socially	Sir George Robinson, Bt Lady Robinson

Baronetesses

There are very few baronetcies (all of them are Scottish) where it is possible for a lady to inherit the title. She is addressed in the same way as a baronet's wife, but note the following.

In writing

Envelope

Where for a baronet the abbreviation Bt would be added, her name should be followed by Btss.

Example Lady Robinson of Glenrobinson, Btss

Husbands should be addressed according to their own rank or title.

Widows of Baronets

Widows of baronets retain their style of address unless and until the succeeding baronet marries, when the widow is called either

> The Dowager Lady Robinson *or*
> Dora, Lady Robinson

The rule follows that of the peerage (*see* page 10).

In speech

Style is the same as for a baronet's wife (*see* page 50).

In writing

Formally

Letter

Madam,
I have the honour to remain,
Your Ladyship's obedient servant,

Less formally

Dear Madam,
Yours faithfully,

Socially

Dear Lady Robinson,
Yours sincerely,

Envelope

The Dowager Lady Robinson *or*
Dora, Lady Robinson

Widows of Baronets Re-marrying

If marrying a peer, an honourable, or another baronet, the title and name of a new husband is taken. If she marries an untitled gentleman, she becomes Mrs . . . . .

Former Wives of Baronets

Until re-marriage they are addressed in the same way as widows, except that they will not be Dowager, but will use a forename before the title.

Children of Baronets

Children of baronets have no titles or distinctions, excepting that the eldest son's forename is not used.

Example Mr Robinson

In Scottish families which have a territorial designation (*see* page 67), he is styled 'younger' (which may be abbreviated yr) of the family description.

Example Mr Robinson, younger of Glenrobinson

Honourables

When the son of a viscount or baron, or the younger son of an earl, receives a baronetcy, the foregoing rules apply, excepting as to the address of envelopes, which should be:

The Hon. Sir George Robinson, Bt
The Hon. Lady Robinson

KNIGHTS AND DAMES

The first rule for all knights or dames who have no other title is that they are addressed as Sir or Lady, with one forename and surname (Sir/Lady Evelyn Brown). The wives of knights are addressed as Lady, with the surname alone (Lady Brown). The husbands of dames are addressed according to their own title or rank.

The orders of knighthood are various, but not one of them is hereditary. We will take them in the order of their precedence and deal with general rules as they arise.

The Most Noble Order of the Garter

This order is conferred most often, but not exclusively, upon royalties and in the peerage. It is distinguished by the letters KG *or* LG after the name and title.

Example The Duke of Middlesex, KG
Lady Susan Braithwaite, LG

The Most Ancient and Most Noble Order of the Thistle

This order is conferred exclusively upon Scottish nobles (these include both peers and certain commoners as nobles in the technical sense) and is distinguished by the letters KT *or* LT after the name and title.

Example The Earl of Queensferry, KT
Sir William MacHector of Drimmore, KT
Lady Margaret Sutherland, LT

The Most Illustrious Order of St Patrick

This order was conferred exclusively upon Irish nobles, and distinguished by the letters KP after the name and title.

Example The Viscount O'Mara, KP

No appointments have been made to the order since 1922.

The Most Honourable Order of the Bath

This is the first of the orders of knighthood in which there is more than one class. Women as well as men are eligible. Members of the first two classes only are knights, and the use of the title in speech and writing is the same as for baronets and their wives and children (except, of course, for the abbreviation Bt). Husbands of ladies raised to any one of the ranks in this order do not share their wives' distinctions.

MEN

Knights

Knights Grand Cross	Sir Robert Johnson, GCB
Knights Commanders	Sir Edward Thompson, KCB

Companions Richard Jackson, Esq., CB

The wives of companions, as such, have no distinctions, though they have recognised precedence.

WOMEN

Dames

Dames Grand Cross	Dame Matilda Johnson, GCB
Dames Commanders	Dame Pamela Thompson, DCB

Companions   Mrs Jackson, CB

The title carried by the first two degrees of this order is used always in conjunction with the lady's forename.

In speech

The formal mode of address is 'Dame Matilda' or 'Dame Pamela'.

In writing   *Letter*

Formally   Madam,

I beg to remain,
Your obedient servant,

Less formally   Dear Madam,
Yours faithfully,

Socially   Dear Dame Matilda Johnson, *or*
Dame Dear Matilda,
Yours sincerely,

Envelope

Dame Matilda Johnson, GCB (or DCB)

Where the recipient of this honour already enjoys a higher title, either by birth or marriage, the accepted rule would seem to be that for a peeress, or the daughter of a duke, marquess, or earl, her title in this order is indicated only by the letters following her name; that the prefix 'The Hon.' should be used with and preceding 'Dame' (as with a knight); and that the wives or widows of baronets and knights may themselves choose whether they wish to be known as, e.g. Lady Jones, DCG, or Dame Bronwen Jones, DCB.

The Most Exalted Order of the Star of India

As in the previous case, this order (which is no longer conferred) has three classes. Members of the first two classes only are knights, and the use of the title in speech and writing is the same as for baronets and their wives and children (excepting, of course, the abbreviation Bt).

Knights Grand Commanders	Sir Robert Johnson, GCSI
Knights Commanders	Sir Edward Thompson, KCSI
Companions	Richard Jackson, Esq., CSI

The wives of companions, as such, have no distinctions, though they have recognised precedence.

The Most Distinguished Order of St Michael and St George

There are three classes in this order, for which women as well as men are eligible. Members of the first two classes only are knights, and the use of the title in speech and writing is the same as for baronets and their wives and children (except, of course, for the abbreviation Bt).

The use of the title carried by the first two degrees of this order (except, of course, that the letters after the name are GCMG or DCMG) is the same as for the Order of the Bath (*see* page 55).

MEN

Knights

Knights Grand Cross	Sir Robert Johnson, GCMG
Knights Commanders	Sir Edward Thompson, KCMG
Companions	Richard Jackson, Esq., CMG

The wives of companions, as such, have no distinctions, though they have recognised precedence.

WOMEN	**Dames**
	The title carried by the first two degrees of this order is used always in conjunction with the lady's forename.

| Dames Grand Cross | Dame Matilda Johnson, GCMG |
| Dames Commanders | Dame Pamela Thompson, DCMG |

Husbands of ladies raised to any one of the ranks in this order do not share their wives' distinctions.

In speech	The formal mode of address is 'Dame Matilda' or 'Dame Pamela'.

In writing	*Letter*
Formally	Madam,
	I beg to remain,
	Your obedient servant,
Less formally	Dear Madam,
	Yours faithfully,
Socially	Dear Dame Matilda Johnson, *or*
	Dear Dame Matilda,
	Yours sincerely,

Envelope

Dame Matilda Johnson, GCMG (or DCMG)

Companions	Mrs Jackson, CMG

The Most Eminent Order of the Indian Empire

There are three classes in this order (which is no longer conferred), members of the first two classes only being knights. The use of the title in speech and writing is the same as for baronets and their wives and children (excepting, of course, the abbreviation Bt). The wives of companions, as such, have no distinctions, though they have recognised precedence.

Knights Grand Commanders	Sir Robert Johnson, GCIE
Knights Commanders	Sir Edward Thompson, KCIE
Companions	Richard Jackson, Esq., CIE

The Royal Victorian Order

There are five classes in this order, for which women as well as men are eligible. Members of the first two classes only are knights, and the use of the title in speech and writing (except, of course, for the abbreviation Bt) is the same as for baronets and their wives and children. The wives of commanders and members, as such, have no distinctions, though they have recognised precedence.

Husbands of ladies raised to any one of the ranks in this order do not share their wives' distinctions.

MEN

Knights

The use of the title carried by the first two degrees of this order (except, of course, that the letters after the name are GCVO or DCVO) is the same as for the Order of the Bath (*see* page 55).

Knights Grand Cross	Sir Robert Johnson, GCVO
Knights Commanders	Sir Edward Thompson, KCVO
Commanders	Richard Jackson, Esq., CVO
Lieutenants	Charles White, Esq., LVO
Members	Herbert Black, Esq., MVO

WOMEN	**Dames**	
	Dames Grand Cross	Dame Matilda Johnson, GCVO
	Dames Commanders	Dame Pamela Thompson, DCVO
	Commanders	Mrs Jackson, CVO
	Lieutenants	Mrs Black, LVO
	Members	Miss Brown, MVO

The Most Excellent Order of the British Empire

This order is the most recent, and women as well as men are eligible.

Members of the first two classes only are knights, and the use of the title in speech and writing (except, of course, the abbreviation Bt) is the same as for baronets and their wives and children. The wives of commanders, officers, and members, as such, have no distinctions, though they have recognised precedence.

Husbands of ladies raised to any one of the ranks in this order do not share their wives' distinctions.

MEN	**Knights**	

The use of the title carried by the first two degrees of this order (except, of course, that the letters after the name are GBE or DBE) is the same as for the Order of the Bath *(see* page 55).

	Knights Grand Cross	Sir Robert Johnson, GBE
	Knights Commanders	Sir Edward Thompson, KBE
	Commanders	Richard Jackson, Esq., CBE

	Officers	Herbert Black, Esq., OBE
	Members	Thomas Brown, Esq., MBE
WOMEN	**Dames**	
	Dames Grand Cross	Dame Matilda Johnson, GBE
	Dames Commanders	Dame Pamela Thompson, DBE
	Commanders	Mrs Jackson, CBE
	Officers	Mrs Black, OBE
	Members	Miss Brown, MBE

Knights Bachelor

This is the lowest order of knighthood, and is designated thus:

Sir William Jones

that is, with forename (not initials) and surname preceded by the title Sir.

Only in formal documents is the word Knight or the abbreviation Kt sometimes added to the name.

It is never correct to use the letters KB to signify a Knight Bachelor. In all other respects the use of the title in speech and writing (except, of course, the abbreviation Bt) is the same as for baronets and their wives and children (*see* pages 50 to 53).

Widows of Knights

No change is made; they continue to be known as Lady . . . . .

Widows of Knights Re-marrying Former Wives of Knights

See under **Baronets** (page 53).

Honorary Orders of Knighthood

See under **Baronets** (page 50).

These are conferred from time to time on foreigners. Except in rare cases granted specially by the Sovereign, the recipient has no right to the title of Sir and it should not be used before the name; but the letters signifying membership of an order may be used after the name, without the abbreviation Hon., e.g.
    Mr Albert C. Gould, KBE.

Knighthoods in Orders not Bestowed by the Crown

Knighthoods in these orders do not confer any title.
    Although appointments in the Most Venerable Order of the Hospital of St John of Jerusalem are gazetted, knights and dames in the order do not receive the accolade. The letters GCStJ, KStJ and DStJ are not used after the name. Papal knighthoods in the orders of St Gregory the Great and St Sylvester also do not confer titles, nor do knighthoods in the Sovereign Military Order of Malta; the abbreviations sometimes seen (GCSG, KSG, KSS, KM, for example) should equally not be used after the name.

General Remarks

All the letters signifying membership of orders, and all decorations, should be used in addressing, subject to the point made below, that a lower rank in an order is absorbed in a higher. These letters are shown in the correct order on page 165.

In the case of a Knight Bachelor being also a companion in another order, his designation would be:

Sir Henry Jones, CB

In this case the letters KCB would be wrong, because, although a knight and a member of the Order of the Bath, he is not a knight in that particular order.

When a member of an order of knighthood is promoted to a higher rank within the same order, the lower rank is absorbed in the higher and therefore the designation of the lower rank is omitted after the name. thus when Richard Jackson, Esq., CVO, is created a knight of the Royal Victorian Order he becomes Sir Richard Jackson, KCVO.

When a son of a viscount or baron or the younger son of an earl receives a knighthood, the foregoing rules apply, excepting as to the address of envelopes, which should be:

The Hon. Sir William Browning, KCMG (or otherwise)
The Hon. Lady Browning

New Titles

All persons awarded orders, decorations, and medals may add the appropriate letters to their names immediately after the announcement in the *London Gazette*, e.g.

John Smith, Esq., CBE
Major Evan Jones, MC
Corporal William Brown, MM

Knights Grand Cross and Knights Commanders of Orders of Chivalry and Knights Bachelor may use the prefix 'Sir' immediately after the official announcement in the *London Gazette*.

Ladies who are appointed Dames Grand Cross or Dames Commanders of Orders of Chivalry may assume the prefix 'Dame' as soon as the notice appears in the *London Gazette*.

The appointment of a Knight or Dame is complete when the accolade is bestowed by the Sovereign. In very rare cases, where personal investiture is impracticable, Letters Patent granting full privileges of the honour are issued.

For procedure in the case of new peerages, *see also* page 7.

SCOTTISH CLANS
and Territorial Houses

By Scots law and custom chiefs of Scottish Clans
and Names, chieftains and lairds are known by
chiefly styles or territorial designations which are
legally part of the surname. Mr is not used and Esq.
seldom.

Chiefs and Chieftains

Examples Mackvicular of Mackvicular is called
Mackvicular in his own territorial district or
gathering, and elsewhere The Mackvicular because
he is chief of the *whole* Name or Clan. (The
Armstrength and The Mackvicular are not
translations of the Gaelic *An*, but a 15th-century
Scots style.)

MacHector of Drimmore is called Drimmore.

In speech   The style is Mackvicular, or Drimmore, *without* Mr
. . . . whatever the rank of the speaker. Their wives
are introduced or announced as:

Mrs Mackvicular of Mackvicular
Mrs MacHector of Drimmore

In writing   *Letter*

Formally   Sir, *or*
Dear Sir,
Yours faithfully,

From a Clansman

Dear Chief,
Yours faithfully,

Socially   Dear Mackvicular,
Yours sincerely, *or*

Dear Drimmore,
Yours sincerely,

In writing

Envelope

The address of envelopes has varied, but since most chiefs were feudal Barons (under Scots law; *see* page 11) who had precedence of ordinary Esquires, the tendency is, again, to omit Esq., and frequently forename, thus:

Examples The Mackvicular of Mackvicular
MacHector of Drimmore
John Brown of Frenchie

English writers who feel uneasy at the omission of Esq. may use it; in this case it *follows* the clan or territorial designation.

Baronets and Knights

Example Sir James MacHector of Drimmore

Service Rank

Example Colonel The Mackvicular, DSO

Any decorations follow the territorial designation.

Wives of Chiefs and Chieftains

Examples The wife of Mackvicular of Mackvicular would be called Mrs Mackvicular *or*
Mrs Mackvicular of Mackvicular.

The wife of MacHector of Drimmore would be called Mrs MacHector.

Wives of chiefs, whether or not they are feudal Barons (under Scots law; *see* page 11) have a legal right to be addressed as Lady if they so wish.

Examples The Lady Mackvicular *or*
The Lady Drimmore.

In writing
Formally

Letter

Madam, *or*
Dear Madam,
Yours faithfully,

Socially

Dear Mrs Mackvicular of Mackvicular, *or*
Dear Mrs MacHector of Drimmore,
Yours sincerely,

Envelope

Mrs Mackvicular of Mackvicular *or*
Mrs MacHector of Drimmore

Widows of Chiefs and Chieftains

The widow of a chief or laird continues to use the territorial style and the prefix Dowager may be used in the same circumstances as where it is applied to a Peeress (*see* page 10).

Example The Dowager Mrs Mackvicular of
Mackvicular

Children of Chiefs and Chieftains

The heirs of chiefs and chieftains are addressed in writing with the distinction 'younger', often abbreviated to 'y', before or after the territorial designation,

Examples John Mackvicular, younger of
Mackvicular
James MacHector of Drimmore, younger

They are also introduced or announced in this way. All unmarried daughters use the title.

Examples Miss MacHector of Drimmore – for the
eldest, and
Miss Jean MacHector of Drimmore – for
a younger one

It is not the custom for younger sons to use the title.

Lairds

The old Scottish title of laird (lord) is still freely used in Scotland, both of the chiefs and chieftains described above and of other landed proprietors.

In rural Scotland their wives are often styled Lady, though not legally except in the case of the wives of chiefs.

Local custom retained these titles, when 'Mrs' was introduced from England towards the close of the 18th century. Technically the 'madam' retained by wives of Irish chieftains is correct, and a few Scottish ones now use it.

Baronets and Knights

Example Sir John Brown of Frenchie

Service Rank

Example Colonel Sir John Brown of Frenchie

IRISH CHIEFTAINRIES
and Knights

Under the Brehon Law, the succession of Irish chieftains was by selection within a limited family group (*deirbhfine*), but the principle of seniority was observed by Gaelic genealogists. About the beginning of the 19th century some of the representatives of the last holders of the chieftainries resumed the appropriate designations, which had lapsed with the destruction of the Gaelic order.

The descent of the following by primogeniture in the male line from the last inaugurated or *de facto* chieftain has been examined by the Genealogical Office, Dublin Castle. Subject to the possible survival in some cases of senior lines at present unidentified, they are recorded at the Genealogical Office as Chiefs of the Name and are recognised by courtesy. Certain chiefs whose pedigrees have not been finally proved are included in this list on account of their prescriptive standing.

Mac Dermot Prince of Coolavin
Mac Gillycuddy of the Reeks
Mac Murrough Kavanagh
O'Brien of Thomond
O'Callaghan
O'Conor Don
O'Donel of Tirconnell
O'Donoghue of the Glens
O'Donovan
O'Morchoe
O'Neill of Clandeboy
O'Sionnaigh (called The Fox since 1552)
O'Toole of Fer Tire
O'Grady of Kilballyowen
O'Kelly of Gallagh and Tycooly

Chieftains

In speech The style is O'Donoghue *without* Mr.

In writing *Letter*

Formally Sir, *or*
Dear Sir,
Yours faithfully,

Socially Dear O'Donoghue,
Yours sincerely,

Envelope

O'Donoghue of the Glens,

or with the prefix The, which, although not officially recognised, is generally used.

Wives of Chieftains

In speech The wife of O'Donoghue referred to and addressed as Madam O'Donoghue.

In writing *Letter*

Formally Madam, *or*
Dear Madam,
Yours faithfully,

Socially Dear Madam O'Donoghue
Yours sincerely,

Envelope

Madam O'Donoghue

Feudal Knights

There are three knights of a palatine creation by an Earl of Desmond in the 14th century: the Knight of Glin, the Knight of Kerry, and the White Knight (this last title is dormant).

In speech	The two holders, both of the Fitzgerald family, are referred to by title and addressed as Knight.
In writing	*Letter*
Formally	Dear Sir, Yours faithfully,
Socially	Dear Knight of Glin, *or* Dear Knight of Kerry, Yours sincerely,

Envelope

The Knight of Glin
The Knight of Kerry, Bt

Wives of Knights

In speech	The wife of the Knight of Glin is addressed as Madam or Madam Fitzgerald. The wife of the Knight of Kerry (who is also a baronet) should be addressed as Lady Fitzgerald.
In writing	*Letter*
Formally	Dear Madam, Yours faithfully,
Socially	Dear Madam Fitzgerald, *or* Dear Lady Fitzgerald,

Envelope

Madam Fitzgerald *or*
Lady Fitzgerald

Joint style on envelope:

The Knight of Glin and Madam Fitzgerald
The Knight of Kerry and Lady Fitzgerald

PRIVY COUNSELLORS

This office is conferred for life, but it is not hereditary. It entitles the holder to the distinction The Right Hon. (in Canada; the Hon.) All members of the British Cabinet must be privy counsellors, but all privy counsellors are not members of the Cabinet. Husbands or wives do not share the title.

In the case of the peerage the office of privy counsellor is not indicated, as in the three lowest grades the title of Right Hon. is already used and in the two highest grades it is assumed to be incorporated in the loftier titles (*see* pages 8–9).

Where there is no other title, the name is preceded by the distinction The Right Hon.

In speech
There is nothing to indicate this rank in the style of addressing, which is according to the holder's rank otherwise.

In writing
Letter

Where there is no other title:

Formally
Sir (or Dear Sir),

I have the honour to be, Sir (or Dear Sir),
Yours faithfully,

Madam, *or*
Dear Madam,

I have the honour to be, Madam (*or* Dear Madam),
Yours faithfully,

Less formally
Dear Sir,
Yours faithfully,

Dear Madam,
Yours faithfully,

In writing	*Letter*
Socially	Dear Mr Williams, Yours sincerely,
	Dear Mrs Johnson, Yours sincerely,

Envelope

The Right Hon. James Williams

Esq. is not used, nor are initials, only forename and surname. His wife would always be addressed as Mrs Williams.

The Right Hon. Matilda Johnson, omitting Mrs or Miss.

Her husband would always be addressed as Esq. unless the envelope is addressed to husband and wife jointly (*see* page 77).

British Navy, Army or Air Force Officers

Envelope

Examples: Admiral The Right Hon. Sir James Smith *or*
Colonel The Right Hon. Henry Jones *or*
Air Vice-Marshal The Right Hon. Sir Josiah Blank

Church dignitaries

Envelope

Example: The Most Rev. and Right Hon. the Lord Archbishop of Blank
The Right Rev. and Right Hon. the Lord Bishop of Blank

ESQUIRES

The use of this title for every man who cannot claim a higher one persists, far more widely than used to be the case, when social usage limited its application to those considered to merit it through social standing, membership of one of the professions, possession of a degree from Oxford or Cambridge University, and so on. It is felt to be courteous in general to use it in all correspondence, although a reaction, influenced by usage in the United States and some other English-speaking countries now leads many writers, especially in business, to prefer the use of Mr.

Whichever style is preferred, it should clearly be used consistently, since the difficulty of ascertaining which of one's correspondents is *entitled* to the appellation Esquire must rule out any thought of using it only where it was, in the past, conferred by social position or other qualification. It should, however, not be used in addressing Quakers, who dislike any form of title.

The title Esquire should never be used in con-junction with any other title, as for instance the prefix Mr.

Example H. J. Robins, Esq.

In speech

The formal manner of address in speech is Sir, and the social manner Mr Robins. His wife or a woman of equal status is called Madam, and referred to as Mrs or Miss Robins.

In writing

Letter

Formally

Sir,
I beg to remain, Sir,
Your obedient servant,

Madam,
I beg to remain, Madam,
Your obedient servant,

In writing	*Letter*
Less formally	Dear Sir, Yours faithfully,
	Dear Madam, Yours faithfully,
Socially	Dear Mr Robins, Yours sincerely,
	Dear Mrs Robins, Yours sincerely,

Envelope

Harold Robins, Esq. *or*
H. J. Robins, Esq.

Mrs Robins, Mrs Harold Robins *or*
Mrs H. J. Robins

(If the person concerned has two or more forenames, it is preferable to use initials; if one only, the name in full.)

For all other male members of the family the rules are the same; envelopes to their wives should include their husbands' forename, for instance:

Mrs John Robins

although this is uncommon in today's usage.

Widows and Former Wives of Esquires

It is wrong to change the form of address on widowhood; Mrs John Robins remains Mrs John Robins when her husband dies, and should not be addressed by her own forename. This error might moreover lead strangers to suppose that her marriage had been dissolved; a former wife would normally use her own forename or initials, thus:

Mrs Mary Robins
Mrs M. A. Robins

Sons of Esquires

Sons bearing the same name or initials as their fathers may be addressed:

Harold Robins, Jnr, Esq.,

if this is necessary to avoid confusion.

There was a Victorian habit of addressing young men of nursery and school age as Master Robins, which seems happily to be dying out. Now the more sensible manner of addressing all boys is simply Harold Robins, until they are old enough for the title Esq.

Daughters of Esquires

The eldest unmarried daughter of the head of the family is Miss Robins. All other unmarried women in the family use their distinguishing forename, for example:

Miss Jane Robins

Orders of Knighthood

Some doubt arises occasionally as to the lesser grades of orders of knighthood. Commanders, Companions, Officers and Members of the various orders of knighthood are addressed as esquires with the distinguishing abbreviation after the name, thus:

Richard Jackson, Esq. CVO

(For fuller details *see under* **Knights** page 54.)

JOINT FORMS OF ADDRESS

It is occasionally necessary to address a letter to husband and wife jointly, although this should be avoided if possible. The only difficulty arises where each spouse is entitled to a different form of address; on these occasions it is necessary to distinguish between them:

Mr and Mrs R. F. Jackson
The Lord and Lady Jackson
but   The Rev. R. F. and Mrs Jackson
Mr R. F. and Rev. Mary Jackson
The Revv. R. F. and Mary Jackson
Sir Richard and Lady Jackson
Mr R. F. and the Hon. Mrs Jackson
Sir Richard Jackson, Bt, and Lady Jackson
The Right Hon. Richard Jackson and Mrs Jackson
Mr R. F. and the Right Hon. Mary Jackson

Where one spouse has honours or decorations indicated by letters after the name these must be shown with the right name:

Colonel R. F. Jackson, CBE, and Mrs Jackson
Sir Richard Jackson and Dame Patricia Jackson, DBE
Mr R. F. Jackson and Dame Mary Jackson, DCMG
Sir Richard Jackson, KBE, and Lady Jackson

See also pages 21, 29, 38, 44 and 49 for the married daughters of peers.

DOUBLE NAMES

The justification for a hyphenated double name is
when two land-owning families have been merged
into one through marriage, or when legal licence to
adopt it has been obtained. The form need not be
denied, however, to those who use a second
forename prefixed to the surname for distinction or
for convenience, though in such cases a hyphen
should not be used. In speech as well as writing the
two names are always used.

PRESIDENTS OF SOCIETIES

The presidents of societies are addressed in formal speech and writing as Sir or Mr President. In the case of a titled holder of the office he would be addressed according to his rank, e.g. My Lord Duke (or Your Grace) and President, or My Lord and President, etc. Where a woman holds office she is addressed as Madam President (except that a duchess would be Your Grace and President). In all cases envelopes are addressed according to name and rank, with the addition of:

President of the . . . . .

THE CHRISTIAN CHURCH:
Church of England

Lords Spiritual

The Archbishops of Canterbury and York, the
Bishops of London, Durham, Winchester and
twenty-one of the other English Diocesan Bishops in
order of seniority of consecration constitute the
Lords Spiritual in Parliament. The Bishop of Sodor
and Man has an honorary seat in the House of Lords
but is a member of the House of Keys, Isle of Man.

Archbishops of Canterbury and York

The Archbishop of Canterbury ranks next in
precedence to the Royal Family, and above the Lord
Chancellor. The Archbishop of York ranks next to
the Lord Chancellor, and above dukes.

Signatures
A reigning archbishop uses his forename in English
or Latin, or the initials of his forenames, coupled
with the Latin name of his see, or some abbreviation
of it. (When the abbreviated Latin name of the see is
used it is usual to put a colon instead of a full stop.)
The Archbishop of Canterbury signs himself (e.g.
Thomas) Cantuar:, and the Archbishop of York signs
(e.g. Henry) Ebor.

In speech

They are referred to as the Archbishop of
Canterbury (*or* York), and not by name. The
manner of addressing by both equals and inferiors
is Your Grace.

In writing	*Letter*
Formally	My Lord Archbishop, *or* Your Grace, I have the honour to remain, my Lord Archbishop, Your Grace's devoted and obedient servant,
Less formally	My Lord Archbishop, Yours faithfully,
Socially	Dear Lord Archbishop, *or* Dear Archbishop, Yours sincerely,

In writing

Envelope

The Archbishops of Canterbury and York, being Privy Counsellors, are addressed as:

The Most Rev. and Right Hon. the Lord Archbishop of Canterbury (*or* York)

Retired Archbishops of Canterbury and York

It has recently been the custom to bestow a temporal peerage upon a retiring Archbishop of Canterbury or upon a retiring Archbishop of York who does not become Archbishop of Canterbury, e.g. Archbishop Lord Coggan, Archbishop Lord Fisher of Lambeth and Archbishop Lord Blanch. They would otherwise renounce their seats in the House of Lords.

Signatures
Retired Archbishops of Canterbury and York use the name that forms part of their temporal title, e.g. Coggan, Fisher of Lambeth and Blanch – according to the usage for temporal peers.

In speech

They are referred to as Archbishop Lord . . . . (see examples above). The manner of addressing is Your Grace or My Lord.

In writing

Letter

Usage is as for reigning archbishops.

Envelope

As Privy Counsellors, they retain the address Right Hon.

The Most Rev. and Right Hon. Lord . . . . *or*
The Right Rev. and Right Hon. Lord . . . .

It is necessary to find out which is preferred.

Other Archbishops of the Anglican Communion

Signatures
The Archbishop of Wales signs himself (e.g. Emrys) Cambrensis, the Archbishop of Armagh signs himself (e.g. James) Armagh, and the Archbishop of Dublin signs himself (e.g. Patrick) Dublin.

In speech

They are referred to by their territorial titles, e.g. the Archbishop of . . . . , and not by name; but where no confusion is likely, 'the Archbishop' is sufficient. The manner of addressing in speech by both equals and inferiors is Your Grace or My Lord.

In writing
Formally
Less formally
Socially

Letter

As for Canterbury and York

Envelope

All archbishops are addressed, both formally and socially as:

The Most Rev. the Lord Archbishop of . . . .

An exception, however, occurs in the case of the Archbishop of Armagh, who is addressed thus:

The Most Rev. His Grace the Lord Primate of All Ireland

Retired Archbishops

On resigning, an archbishop, though relinquishing his legal, constitutional and ecclesiastical status as archbishop, remains a bishop, and should in principle be addressed as Right Reverend rather than Most Reverend. By courtesy, nevertheless (or by habit), he may still be addressed as archbishop; unless, having perhaps held archiepiscopal office overseas, he should be appointed as a bishop in this country, when he will be addressed as a bishop. This will be so if the appointment be as diocesan, suffragan or assistant bishop, according to the rule for each.

Signatures
Retired archbishops use their ordinary signatures, with the addition of Archbishop or Bishop.

In speech
Retired archbishops are referred to in speech, both socially and formally, by title and surname; it is again necessary to discover whether Archbishop, or Bishop, is preferred. The manner of address in conversation is My Lord.

In writing *Letter*

Formally
My Lord, *or*
My Lord Bishop, *or*
My Lord Archbishop (where this form is retained),
I have the honour to remain, My Lord (*or* as above),
Your devoted and obedient servant,

Less formally
My Lord,
Yours faithfully,

Socially
Dear Lord Bishop, *or*
Dear Bishop, *or*
Dear Archbishop,
Yours sincerely,

Envelope

The Right Rev. John Brown *or*
The Most Rev. John Brown

There is no alternative to discovering which form is preferred in each case.

Wives of Archbishops

Being wife to an archbishop confers no precedence or special title. A wife is plain Mrs unless she has a title of her own or her husband has a temporal title.

Bishops

All the bishops of the Anglican Communion have come by custom or right to be styled Lord Bishops. From time immemorial the Episcopal character and office have attracted forms of address of the highest dignity and reverence. Their variable forms have taken their present shape of Lord Bishop, a title which may be used with propriety of all episcopally consecrated bishops. Though in the Eastern churches titles more splendid and picturesque are in use, Lord Bishop is never wrong.

The title 'Lord Bishop' is not confined to those English diocesan bishops who happen by reason of seniority to have seats in the House of Lords. All diocesan bishops of England are described in legal documents as Lord Bishops. The title owes nothing to special grant or to any act of sovereignty by monarch. Nor can the title be traced to the fact that bishops were formerly barons also, possessing land and revenues accordingly. The title *Dominus Episcopus* was in use before the Conquest and before the bishops were constituted barons.

The twenty-four English bishops who, with the two archbishops, have seats in the House of Lords, rank below viscounts and above barons.

In speech	The manner of address in speech is My Lord and His Lordship, both formally and socially.
In writing	*Letter*
Formally	My Lord, *or*
	My Lord Bishop,
	I have the honour to remain,
	Your Lordship's obedient servant,
Less formally	My Lord,
	Yours faithfully,
Socially	Dear Lord Bishop, *or* Dear Bishop,
	Yours sincerely,
	Envelope
	The Right Rev. the Lord Bishop of . . . .

Bishops Suffragan

In the United Kingdom they are not addressed as such but by courtesy exactly as diocesan bishops; they are styled Bishop of . . . . , not Bishop Suffragan of whatever the diocese may be. (*Example* The Bishops Suffragan of Grantham and Grimsby are addressed as though they were diocesan bishops of sees of these names, and not as Bishops Suffragan in the diocese of Lincoln.)

In Canada and Australia, however, although they may (particularly in Canada) be given a territorial style of their own, they are thought of and addressed as suffragans of the diocese:

The Right Rev. the Suffragan Bishop of . . . .

Bishops of the Anglican Communion

In speech and writing

The manner of address in speech and writing, both formally and socially, is exactly the same as for English bishops. There are, however, the following minor points of distinction to be borne in mind.

Irish Bishops

In speech and writing

The manner of address in speech and writing is the same as for English bishops.

The exception is the Bishop of Meath, who is addressed as 'The Most Rev.' instead of 'The Right Rev.', as Premier Bishop of the Church of Ireland.

Scottish Bishops

The same as for Irish bishops (*see above*). One bishop is elected as Primus who is addressed in speech and writings as 'My Lord' or 'My Lord Primus'.

In writing

Envelope

The Most Rev. the Primus

Elsewhere

In speech and writing

Some bishops discourage the use of the title – this is their preference. Until lately the title has been unknown in the American Episcopal Church, so far as domestic use is concerned, but American bishops should in courtesy be addressed by English-speaking correspondents outside the USA in the manner applicable to all other bishops of the Anglican Communion. The American style 'Right Reverend Sir' is, indeed, giving place occasionally to 'My Lord' in USA.

Bishops Coadjutor

In speech and writing

In the Anglican church overseas Bishops Coadjutor may be appointed to assist an Archbishop. They have no separate territorial style, and are addressed by name, with the addition of their office:

The Right Rev. A. B. . . . . . ,
Bishop Coadjutor of . . . . .

Assistant Bishops

In speech and writing

In Britain Assistant Bishops may be appointed, after retirement as a diocesan or suffragan, to assist the bishop of the diocese in which they are living. They are addressed by name. In the Anglican church overseas this title may be given to younger men who after consecration are appointed to assist the bishop of a large diocese. The form of address is the same in either case:

The Right Rev. C. D. . . . .

Retired Bishops

In speech

Retired bishops are addressed by their names, but otherwise as for English bishops.

In writing
Formally
Less formally
Socially

Letter

As for English bishops

Envelope
The Right Rev. John Brown

Wives of Bishops

As for the wives of archbishops, no precedence or special title is conferred. A wife is plain Mrs unless she has a title of her own or her husband has a temporal title.

Deans

In speech

The style of address is Mr Dean or Dean.

In writing	*Letter*
Formally	Very Reverend Sir,
	I have the honour to remain, Very Reverend Sir, Your obedient servant,
Less formally	but on a church matter:
	Dear Sir,
	Yours faithfully,
Socially	Dear Mr Dean, *or* Dear Dean,
	Yours sincerely,

Envelope

The Very Rev. the Dean of . . . .

Deans who are also Bishops are addressed as The Right Rev. the Dean of . . . .

Retired Deans

Retired deans have no right to the title on retirement, and are addressed as other members of the clergy (*see* page 91), but if the title Dean Emeritus is conferred they are addressed as deans (also, by courtesy, if it is known that they wish to retain the title), except that the envelope would be addressed in the personal name, thus:

The Very Rev. Charles Cox

Provosts

Provosts are the incumbents of those parish churches which have become cathedrals in recent times. They take rank and precedence as deans.

In speech   They are addressed as Mr Provost or Provost.

In writing	*Letter*
Formally	Very Reverend Sir,
	I have the honour to remain, Very Reverend Sir, Your obedient servant,
Less formally	but on a church matter:
	Dear Sir, Yours faithfully,
Socially	Dear Mr Provost, *or* Dear Provost, Yours sincerely,

Envelope

The Very Rev. the Provost of . . . .

Retired Provosts

Rules as for retired deans apply.

Archdeacons

In speech	They are addressed as Archdeacon.
In writing	*Letter*
Formally	Venerable Sir *or* Madam,
	I have the honour to remain, Venerable Sir *or* Madam, Your obedient servant,
Less formally	but on a church matter:
	Dear Sir *or* Madam, Yours faithfully,
Socially	Dear Archdeacon, Yours sincerely,

Envelope

The Venerable the Archdeacon of . . . .

Retired Archdeacons

Retired archdeacons have no right to the title on retirement, and are addressed as other members of the clergy (see page 91), but if the title Archdeacon Emeritus is conferred on them (also, by courtesy, if it is known that they wish to retain the title), they are addressed in speech as Archdeacon and referred to as Archdeacon . . . . (surname), except in official documents. The envelope would be addressed:

The Venerable Arthur Holt

Canons

Canons are either residentiary or honorary. The rule is the same in each case.

In speech   They are addressed as Canon . . . . (surname).

In writing   *Letter*

Formally   Reverend Sir *or* Madam,

I have the honour to remain, Reverend Sir *or* Madam,
Your obedient servant,

Less formally   but on a church matter:

Dear Sir *or* Madam,
Yours faithfully,

Socially   Dear Canon, *or*
Dear Canon . . . . (surname),
Yours sincerely,

Envelope

The Rev. Canon . . . . (christian name and surname)

Minor canons are addressed as other members of the clergy, with no special title.

Prebendaries

In speech	Prebendaries are addressed as Prebendary . . . .
In writing	*Letter*
Formally	Reverend Sir,
	I have the honour to be, Reverend Sir,
	Your obedient servant,
Less formally	but on a church matter:
	Dear Sir,
	Yours faithfully,
Socially	Dear Prebendary, *or*
	Dear Prebendary . . . . ,
	Yours sincerely,
	Envelope
	The Rev. Prebendary . . . .

Other Members of the Clergy

There is no difference in style of addressing the remaining ranks, although beneficed clergy are usually called in speech either The Rector or The Vicar. But it is definitely wrong to refer or write to the Rev. Smith. Initials or forename must *always* be used, unless they are not known.

The style Rev. Mr Smith was once common in England but its use is now confined to North America, where it is correct.

In speech	They are addressed as Vicar, Rector *or* Mr *or* Mrs, Miss . . . .
In writing	*Letter*
Formally	Reverend Sir/Madam, *or*
	Sir/Madam,
	I beg to remain, Reverend Sir/Madam (*or* Sir/Madam),
	Your obedient servant,

Less formally	Dear Sir *or* Madam, Yours faithfully,
Socially	Dear Mr *or* Mrs, Miss Smith, *or* Dear Rector (or Vicar), Yours sincerely,

Envelope

The Rev. A. B. Smith

When the name of a clergyman and his wife appear together, the correct form is:

The Rev. A. B. and Mrs Smith

Titled Clerics

A temporal title is always preceded in writing by the spiritual one.

Examples   The Right Rev. and Right Hon. the Lord Bishop of London
The Rev. Lord John Smith
The Rev. The Hon. David Jones
The Rev. Sir John Bull, Bt

No ordained priest of the Church can receive the accolade of knighthood, but in some cases an appointment to an order of knighthood is made which carries the designation (e.g. KCVO) without the title. The initials follow the name in the usual way:

The Right Rev. John Brown, KCVO,

or, where the see rather than the name is used:

The Right Rev. the Lord Bishop of . . . . , KCVO

The wife of a priest so honoured is not styled or addressed Lady unless she is already entitled to such designation.

Anglican Religious Communities

MEN	**Head of community**
In speech	Father Abbot *or* Father Prior *or* Father Superior
In writing	*Letter*

Dear Abbot (*or* Prior *or* Superior),
Yours faithfully,

Envelope

The Right Rev. the Lord Abbot *or*
The Rev. the Prior *or*
The Rev. (*or* The Rev. Father) Superior

The initials of the community (should it use them)
are added immediately after the name, even if there
are decorations or degrees as well.

Ordained Members of a Community

In speech   Father *or* (in Franciscan Communities) Brother

In writing   *Letter*

Dear Rev. Father,
Yours faithfully,

Envelope

The Rev. (*or* The Rev. Father) A. B. Smith, SSJE
The Rev. (*or* The Rev. Father) J. L. Read, CR, DD

Lay Members of Community

In speech   Brother John

In writing   *Letter*

Dear Brother John,
Yours faithfully,

Envelope

Brother John Green

Benedictines

Whether ordained or lay, Benedictines are addressed as Dom:

The Rev. Dom James Martin, OSB *or*
Dom James Martin, OSB, if a lay member

WOMEN

In speech

Head of Community

Reverend Mother (in some Communities, Mother) *or* Sister

In writing

Letter

Dear Reverend Mother *or* Sister,
Yours faithfully,

Envelope

The Rev. The Prioress *or*
The Rev. Mother Superior

Ordinary Members of Community

In speech

Sister Mary

In writing

Letter

Dear Sister Mary,
Yours faithfully,

Envelope

Sister Mary Brown
followed by the initials of the Community.

Benedictines

Benedictines are addressed as Dame:

Dame Mary Brown, OSB

Chancellors

Chancellors are the judges of the Episcopal Courts and the principal lay officers of the respective dioceses. They are usually, but not invariably, barristers. The title is used only in connection with official duties.

In speech

By the clergy and others within the diocese:

Mr Chancellor, *or,* more familiarly, Chancellor

Madam Chancellor

In court:

Sir, Worshipful Sir (not Your Worship) and The Learned Chancellor are correct.

Madam, Worshipful Madam

In writing

Letter

Formally

Sir (*or* Dear Sir),

Madam (*or* Dear Madam),

Less formally

Dear Mr Chancellor,

Dear Madam Chancellor,

Envelope

The Worshipful Chancellor Smith *or*
The Worshipful Thomas Smith *or*
The Worshipful Sir Thomas Smith (if a knight)

The Worshipful Alice Jones *or*
The Worshipful Lady Alice Jones

If the chancellor is a QC the initials should come after the name.

Chancellors of Cathedrals

Chancellors of cathedrals are clergymen and should be addressed by clerical title.

THE CHRISTIAN CHURCH: Church of Scotland

The Lord High Commissioner to the General Assembly

In speech

He is addressed and referred to as Your Grace and His Grace. Only during his term of office is he entitled to any special form of address.

In writing

Letter

Formally and socially

Your Grace,

Your Grace's most devoted and obedient servant,

When the office is held by a member of the Royal Family, the formal and social address may be either Your Royal Highness or Your Grace.

Envelope

His Grace the Lord High Commissioner

The Moderator

In speech

He is addressed as Moderator, *or* as Dr . . . . (or Mr . . . . , as the case may be).

In writing

Letter

Formally

Right Reverend Sir,

I beg to remain, Right Reverend Sir,
Your obedient servant,

Less formally

Dear Sir, *or*
Dear Moderator,
Yours faithfully,

Socially

Dear Moderator, *or*
Dear Dr (or Mr) Smith,
Yours sincerely,

In writing	*Envelope*
	The Right Rev. the Moderator of the General Assembly of the Church of Scotland

Ex-Moderators

These dignitaries are designated The Very Reverend.

In speech	They are addressed as Dr . . . . (*or* Mr . . . .).
In writing	*Letter*
Formally	Very Reverend Sir, I beg to remain, Very Reverend Sir, Your obedient servant,
Less formally	Dear Sir, *or* Dear Minister, Yours faithfully,
Socially	Dear Dr (or Mr) Smith, Yours sincerely,

Envelope

The Very Rev. Albert Smith (and if a Dr), DD.

Other Members of the Clergy

Rules as for the Church of England apply (*see* page 91), except that the titles of Vicar and Rector are not used. A minister in a regular parochial charge is often called The Minister (of the parish) or the Parish Minister, and addressed as Dr . . . . (surname) *or* Mr *or* Mrs, Miss . . . . (surname). Envelopes are addressed The Minister of . . . .

Dean of the Thistle and Chapel Royal

Rules as for Deans of the Church of England apply here (*see* page 87).

THE CHRISTIAN CHURCH:
Roman Catholic Church

It should be understood that the following rules have no legal foundation in this country. Roman Catholic archbishops and bishops have no claim to territorial titles or to the use of the salutations Your Grace or My Lord, and such modes of address are not permitted in official documents and circles. But unofficially and within the Roman Catholic community this chapter holds good.

The Pope

The Pope is the supreme head on earth of the Roman Catholic Church,

In speech

He is personally addressed and referred to as Your Holiness or His Holiness.

In writing

Letter

Formally

Your Holiness,

I have the honour to remain,
Your Holiness's most devoted and obedient child,

or

Most Holy Father,
Your Holiness's most humble child,

A non-Roman Catholic may subscribe himself 'servant' and not 'child'.

Envelope

His Holiness The Pope

Letters addressed to the Pope would normally go through ecclesiastical channels, and if written in English would be translated into Latin.

Cardinals

In speech

Cardinals are addressed and referred to both formally and socially as Your Eminence and His Eminence.

In writing

Letter

Formally

My Lord Cardinal, *or*
Your Eminence,

I have the honour to remain, my Lord Cardinal, Your Eminence's devoted and obedient child,

A non-Roman Catholic may subscribe himself 'servant' and not 'child'.

Less formally

Your Eminence,
I remain, Your Eminence,
Yours faithfully,

Socially

Dear Cardinal . . . . ,
Yours sincerely,

Envelope

His Eminence Cardinal . . . . .

Cardinal Archbishops and Cardinal Bishops

Rules as for Cardinals apply here, except as to the address of envelope, which should be:

His Eminence the Cardinal Archbishop of . . . .

or, preferably

His Eminence Cardinal . . . . , Archbishop of
. . . . .

since the dignity of Cardinal is personal, and not attached to the office of Archbishop. The same rule should be followed for Cardinals who are Bishops.

Archbishops

In speech

Archbishops are addressed and referred to in speech both formally and socially as Your Grace and His Grace.

In writing   *Letter*

Formally

My Lord Archbishop, *or*
Your Grace,

I have the honour to remain, my Lord Archbishop, Your Grace's devoted and obedient child,

A non-Roman Catholic may subscribe himself 'servant' and not 'child'.

Less formally

Your Grace,
Yours faithfully,

Socially

Dear Archbishop,
Yours sincerely,

Envelope

His Grace The Archbishop of . . . . *or*
The Most Rev. James Smith, Archbishop of . . . .

The Archbishop of Armagh is the Primate of All Ireland, and the Archbishop of Dublin is the Primate of Ireland. In these cases the following form is appropriate:

The Most Rev. James Smith
Archbishop of Armagh and Primate of All Ireland

The Most Rev. James Smith
Archbishop of Dublin and Primate of Ireland

Form used within British Commonwealth

In writing   *Letter*

Most Reverend Sir,
I (We) have the honour to be,
Your faithful servant(s),

Envelope

The Most Rev. Archbishop Brown

Retired Archbishops

In writing	*Envelope*
	The Most Rev. Archbishop Smith

Bishops

In speech	The manner of address both formally and socially is My Lord and His Lordship.
In writing	*Letter*
Formally	My Lord, *or*
	My Lord Bishop,
	I have the honour to remain,
	Your Lordship's obedient child (or servant),
Less formally	My Lord,
	Yours faithfully,
Socially	Dear Bishop,
	Yours sincerely,

Envelope

The Right Rev. James Smith, Bishop of . . . .
or His Lordship the Bishop of . . . .

Form used within British Commonwealth

In writing	*Letter*
	Right Reverend Sir,
	I (We) have the honour to be,
	Your faithful servant(s),

Envelope

The Right Rev. Bishop Brown

Irish Bishops

The foregoing rules apply, except that the envelope is addressed:

The Most Rev. the Bishop of . . . .

Other English-Speaking Countries

Bishops in other English-speaking countries are
customarily also addressed as Most Rev.

Retired Bishops

In writing

Envelope

The Right Rev. Bishop Smith

Bishops Coadjutor

**In speech and
writing**

Bishops Coadjutor are appointed to assist a bishop
or archbishop, and will normally succeed him on his
retirement. They are addressed as bishops, but are
referred to and addressed on envelopes by personal
name.

Example The Right Rev. William Flynn, Bishop
Coadjutor of . . . .

Bishops Auxiliary

**In speech and
writing**

Bishops Auxiliary are also appointed to assist an
archbishop or a bishop, but without the expectation
of succession. They are addressed as bishops, but are
referred to and addresses on envelopes by personal
name.

Example The Right Rev. John Haines, Bishop
Auxiliary of . . . .

Titular Sees

A titular see is an honorary title for a bishop who
has no see or an honorary additional title for a
bishop who has one.

In writing	Foregoing rules for Archbishops and Bishops apply, except as to envelopes, which are addressed:
	The Most Rev. Archbishop Brown The Right Rev. (*or* Most Rev.) Bishop Brown
	It is unnecessary to refer to the titular see.

Provosts

In speech	They are addressed as Provost . . . .
In writing	*Letter*
Formally	Very Reverend Sir, I have the honour to remain, Very Reverend Sir, Your obedient servant,
Less formally	Dear Sir, Your faithfully,
Socially	Dear Provost . . . . . , *or* Dear Provost, Yours sincerely,
	Envelope The Very Rev. Provost . . . . .

Canons

In speech	Canons are addressed and referred to as Canon . . . . .
In writing	*Letter*
Formally	Very Reverend Sir, I have the honour to remain, Very Reverend Sir, Your obedient servant,
Less formally	Dear Sir, Yours faithfully,

In writing	*Letter*
Socially	Dear Canon . . . . , *or*
	Dear Canon,
	Yours sincerely,

Envelope

The Very Rev. Canon . . . .

If he is a Monsignore, this is added: The Very Rev. Monsignor (Canon) . . . . . Both titles may be used, but it is unnecessary.

Monsignori

Monsignori may be Protonotaries, Domestic Prelates, Privy Chamberlains, or Honorary Chamberlains of His Holiness the Pope.

In speech	They are addressed and referred to both formally and socially, as Monsignor Smith, or as Monsignore.
In writing	*Letter*
Formally	Reverend Sir,
	I have the honour to remain, Reverend Sir,
	Your devoted and obedient servant,
Less formally	Reverend Sir,
	Yours faithfully,
Socially	Dear Monsignore, *or*
	Dear Monsignor Smith,
	Yours sincerely,

Envelope

The Rev. Mgr Vincent Smith, *or*
The Rev. Monsignore

Priests

In speech	Priests are addressed and referred to as Father . . .

In writing	*Letter*
Formally	Dear Reverend Father, Your devoted and obedient child (or servant),
Less formally	Dear Reverend Father, Yours faithfully,
Socially	Dear Father . . . . , Yours sincerely,

Envelope

The Rev. Father . . . . .

Titled Priests

As with the clergy of the Church of England (*see* page 92), the spiritual title always precedes the temporal one.

Roman Catholic clergy do, however, use the title Sir if they become a member of an order of knighthood; the former Archbishop of Sydney, for example, was known as His Eminence Sir Norman Cardinal Gilroy, KBE.

Roman Catholic Religious Communities

Provincials

In speech	Provincials are addressed and referred to as Father . . . . .
In writing	*Letter*
Formally	Very Reverend Father, I beg to remain, Very Reverend Father, Your devoted and obedient child (or servant),
Less formally	Very Reverend Father, Yours faithfully,

In writing	*Letter*
Socially	Dear Father . . . . , *or* Dear Father Provincial, Yours sincerely,
	Envelope
	The Very Rev. Father . . . . , *or* The Very Rev. Father Provincial (with distinguishing initials of his order)

MEN **Heads of Community: Abbots, et al.**

In speech Abbots are addressed and referred to as Father Abbot.

In writing	*Letter*
Formally	My Lord Abbot, *or* Right Reverend Abbot . . . , *or* Right Reverend Father, I beg to remain, my Lord Abbot (or alternatives), Your devoted and obedient servant,
Less formally	My Lord Abbot, Yours faithfully,
Socially	Dear Father Abbot, Yours sincerely,
	Envelope
	The Right Rev. the Abbot of Thornton (with distinguishing initials of his order)
	Benedictine Abbots do not use the designation 'Lord Abbot'.

Ordained Members of Community

See **Priests** on page 104.

Lay Members of Community

Lay members are addressed as Brother . . . . .

Benedictines

Whether ordained or lay, Benedictines are addressed as Dom:

In writing	*Envelope*
	The Rev. Dom Henry Smith, OSB *or*
	Dom Henry Smith, OSB, if a lay member

WOMEN

Heads of Community

The head of a community may be called Abbess, Prioress, Superior or Reverend Mother.

In speech

She should be addressed as Reverend Mother if not established otherwise.

In writing

Letter

Dear Lady Abbess,
Dear Reverend Mother,
Dear Sister Superior,
Yours faithfully,

Envelope

She will be addressed according to her office, with the addition of the letters of her order:

The Lady Abbess
The Reverend Mother Prioress
The Reverend Mother
The Mother Superior
The Sister Superior

Other Members of Community

In speech and writing

Other members of the order are addressed as The Reverend Sister, with forename, or Christian and surname, according to the custom of the order and, on an envelope, with the letters of the order, if used.

Benedictines

Benedictines are addressed as Dame:
Dame Margaret Jones, OSB

Chancellors

They are diocesan archivists or confidential secretaries to bishops.

THE CHRISTIAN CHURCH:
Free Churches

Ministers

In speech

Ministers are addressed as Dr . . . . (*or* Mr . . . . Mrs . . . . , or Miss . . . .).

In writing

Letter

Formally

Dear Sir, *or*
Dear Madam, *or*
Dear Minister,
Yours faithfully,

Socially

Dear Dr (*or* Mr, Mrs, or Miss) Smith,
Yours sincerely,

Envelope

The Rev. Matthew Smith *or*
The Rev. Margaret Smith

'The Rev. Smith' is in all cases incorrect, and 'Rev. Smith' even more so.

Retired Ministers and Other Clergy

The form of address is the same as for Ministers but without the term Minister being used.

THE CHRISTIAN CHURCH:
Other Denominations

As a matter of courtesy, rules as for Other Clergy of the Church of England apply (*see* page 91).

THE CHRISTIAN CHURCH:
Eastern Church

Patriarchs

In speech

Patriarchs are personally addressed and referred to as Your Holiness or His Holiness.

In writing

Letter

Your Holiness,
I have the honour to be, Sir,
Your Holiness's obedient servant,

Envelope

His Holiness The Patriarch

Metropolitans

In speech

Metropolitans are personally addressed and referred to as Your Grace and His Grace.

In writing

Letter

Your Grace,
I am, Sir,
Your Grace's obedient servant,

Envelope

His Beatitude The Metropolitan of . . . .

Archbishops and Bishops

As for Anglican Archbishops and Bishops (*see* pages 83 and 85).

Archimandrites

In speech	Archimandrites are addressed and referred to in speech as Right Reverend Father.
In writing	*Letter*
Formally	Right Reverend Father,
	I beg to remain, Right Reverend Father, Your obedient servant,
Socially	Dear Father, Yours sincerely,
	Envelope
	The Right Rev. Father . . . . .

THE JEWISH SYNAGOGUE

The Chief Rabbi

In speech   He is addressed and referred to as Chief Rabbi.

In writing   *Letter*
Formally   Very Reverend and dear Sir,
                         I am, Very Reverend Sir,
                         Your obedient servant,

Less formally   Dear Sir,
                         Yours faithfully,

Socially   Dear Chief Rabbi,
                         Yours sincerely,

                         Envelope
                         The Very Rev. the Chief Rabbi *or*
                         The Chief Rabbi Dr J. Cohen

Rabbis

In speech   Rabbis are addressed and referred to in speech as
                         Rabbi Cohen.

In writing   *Letter*
Formally   Reverend and dear Sir *or* Madam,
                         I am, Reverend Sir,
                         Your obedient servant,

Less formally   Dear Sir *or* Madam,
                         Yours faithfully,

Socially   Dear Rabbi Cohen,
                         Yours sincerely,

                         Envelope
                         The Rev. Rabbi A. Cohen

Rabbi Doctors

In speech	Rabbi Doctors are addressed and referred to as Dr Cohen.
In writing	*Letter*
Formally	Dear Sir *or* Madam, Yours faithfully,
Socially	Dear Dr Cohen, Yours sincerely,

Envelope

The Rev. Rabbi Dr A. Cohen

Ministers

In speech	Ministers are addressed and referred to as Mr, Mrs or Miss Cohen or Dr Cohen, according to degree.
In writing	*Letter*
Formally	Reverend and dear Sir *or* Madam, I am, Reverend Sir *or* Madam, Your obedient servant,
Less formally	Dear Sir, Yours faithfully,
Socially	Dear Mr, Mrs, Miss (*or* Dr) Cohen, Yours sincerely,

Envelope

The Rev. A. Cohen *or*
The Rev. Dr A. Cohen

OTHER FAITHS

Many faiths are now practised for which no indisputable body of conventions exists in the United Kingdom. Muslims, Hindus, Sikhs, Buddhists and adherents of other religions have a variety of religious and cultural organisations which have different hierarchies.

It is recommended that an approach be made to places of worship or to cultural centres to ascertain the modes deemed most appropriate for individual priests, ministers and officials.

THE ARMED FORCES:
Comparative Ranks

Royal Navy	Royal Marines	Army	Royal Air Force
Admiral of the Fleet	Captain-General	Field-Marshal	Marshal of the Royal Air Force
Admiral	General	General	Air Chief Marshal
Vice-Admiral	Lieutenant-General	Lieutenant-General	Air Marshal
Rear-Admiral	Major-General	Major-General	Air Vice-Marshal
Commodore RN (senior captains)	Colonel	Brigadier	Air Commodore
Captain RN	Lieutenant-Colonel RM	Colonel	Group Captain RAF
Commander RN	Major RM	Lieutenant-Colonel	Wing Commander
Lieutenant Commander RN	Captain RM	Major	Squadron Leader RAF
Lieutenant RN	Lieutentant RM	Captain	Flight Lieutenant
Sub-Lieutenant RN	Second Lieutenant RM	Lieutenant	Flying Officer RAF
		Second Lieutenant	Pilot Officer RAF

Womens Royal Naval Service (WRNS)	Womens Royal Army Corps (WRAC)	Womens Royal Air Force (WRAF)
Chief Commandant	Major-General	Air Marshal
Commandant	Brigadier	Air Commodore
Superintendent	Colonel	Group Captain
Chief Officer	Lieutenant-Colonel	Wing Commander
First Officer	Major	Squadron Leader
Second Officer	Captain	Flight Lieutenant
Third Officer	Lieutenant	Flying Officer
	Second Lieutenant	Pilot Officer

THE ARMED FORCES:
Royal Navy

This is the senior fighting service. For all ranks below Rear-Admiral, the words Royal Navy, or more usually in ordinary correspondence the abbreviation RN will be added after the name, and any decorations and orders.

Decorations and honours should never be omitted from envelopes.

A few general rules are given below.

In speech

All ranks above that of sub-lieutenant are addressed and referred to by their service title (unless they possess a higher title otherwise).

Admirals of the Fleet

Admirals of the Fleet will normally be holders of some other title.

In writing

Letter

According to peerage or other rank.

Envelope

Formally and socially

Admiral of the Fleet Lord (or any other title) . . . . . .

Admirals
Vice-Admirals
Rear-Admirals

In speech

All are addressed as Admiral . . . .

In writing

Letter

Formally

Sir,

I have the honour to remain, Sir,
Your obedient servant,

In writing	*Letter*
Less formally	Dear Sir, Yours faithfully,
Socially	The social manner is by his title if he has one, otherwise:
	Dear Admiral Flint, Yours sincerely,
	Officers of this rank may express a preference for being addressed by rank rather than by title; if so, their preference should be followed.

Envelope

Only on envelopes are the graded service titles used.

Commodores

The rank is held by senior captains in special appointments.

In speech	The title is used with the surname both formally and socially.

In writing	*Letter*
Formally	Sir, I have the honour to be, Sir, Your obedient servant,
Less formally	Dear Sir, Yours faithfully,
Socially	Dear Commodore Beal, Yours sincerely,

Envelope

Commodore A. Beal, Royal Navy (or RN)

Captains

In speech	The title is used with the surname both formally and socially.

In writing	*Letter*
Formally	Sir,
	I have the honour to be, Sir,
	Your obedient servant,
Less formally	Dear Sir,
	Yours faithfully,
Socially	Dear Captain Birch,
	Yours sincerely,

Envelope

Captain A. B. Birch, Royal Navy (or RN)

Commanders

In speech This title is used with the surname both formally and socially.

In writing *Letter*

As for Captains, with the title Commander used for social address.

Envelope

Commander C. D. Bartlett, Royal Navy (*or* RN)

Lieutenant-Commanders

In speech They are addressed as Commander with the surname.

In writing *Letter*

As for Captains, with the title Commander used for social address.

Envelope (only here is graded title used.)

Lieutenant-Commander C. D. Bartlett,
Royal Navy (*or* RN)

Lieutenants

In speech	They are addressed officially as Lieutenant and socially as Mr – both with the surname.
In writing	*Letter*
	As for Captains, with the title Lieutenant used for social address.
	Envelope
	Lieutenant G. H. Crane, Royal Navy (*or* RN)

Sub-Lieutenants
Midshipmen
Cadets

In speech	All are addressed officially and socially as Mr, with the surname.
In writing	*Letter*
	All are addressed as Mr, with the surname.
	Envelope
Formally and socially	Sub-Lieut I. J. Drake, Royal Navy (*or* RN)
	Midshipman K. L. Blake, Royal Navy (*or* RN)
	Cadet M. N. Hawke, Royal Navy (*or* RN)

General List

The foregoing rules apply to all officers on the General List (i.e. Seaman, Engineering, Electrical Engineering, and Supply & Secretariat specialists).

Medical Officers

In speech	Medical Officers should be addressed by rank, prefixed by the name of their branch when referred to.

In writing

Letter

The foregoing rules apply.

Envelope

Surgeon-Commander S. T. Brice, RN

Chaplains

The Chaplain of the Fleet is an Archdeacon, and is addressed accordingly (*see* page 89) in speech and letter. The envelope may be addressed to The Chaplain of the Fleet, or with this designation added to the name.

Other chaplains are addressed as clergymen with the words Royal Navy or the initials RN attached to their names.

Titled Officers

A hereditary or conferred title is preceded by the naval one.

Examples Admiral Sir Norman Blake
Captain the Hon. Norman Birch, Royal Navy (*or* RN)

Retired Officers

A retired officer of the rank of lieutenant-commander or above should be addressed in exactly the same way as one of the active list, except that the abbreviation 'Rtd' should be added whenever it is necessary to indicate the fact. For instance, a private letter should be addressed without the suffix, but a letter to a retired officer working, say in the Ministry of Defence, or for a ship-builder, should add 'Rtd'.

Decorations

Abbreviations are used immediately after the name thus:

Captain O. P. Hawke, DSO, Royal Navy
Lieut A. R. Crane, DSC, Royal Navy

They should, of course, never be omitted.

Royal Naval Volunteer Reserve

Usage is similar to that for professional members of the Royal Navy but forms of address should be employed only on naval business.

THE ARMED FORCES:
Royal Marines

Officers of the Royal Marines have Army ranks although they are more closely connected with the Royal Navy.

In speech

Forms of address are the same as for the Army (*see* pages 122–25).

In writing

Letter

Forms of address are the same as for the Army (*see* pages 122–25).

Envelope

The letters RM should follow the surname if the rank is Lieutenant-Colonel or below.

Captain-General

It will be noted from the table of comparative ranks on page 114 that the highest rank is that of Captain-General, and not Field-Marshal as in the Army. Any holder of this position will normally possess some other title and will be addressed accordingly.

THE ARMED FORCES: Army

All ranks above that of lieutenant are addressed and referred to in speech by their service title (unless they possess a higher one otherwise). Decorations and honours should never be omitted from envelopes.

Field-Marshals

In speech

Field-Marshals will normally be holders of some other title and will be addressed accordingly.

In writing

Letter

According to peerage or other rank.

Envelope

Field-Marshal Lord (*or* any other title) . . . . .

Generals
Lieutenant-Generals
Major-Generals

In speech

All are addressed as General . . . .

In writing

Letter

Formally and socially

The formal manner of address is Sir, the social manner is Dear General Sands, or by his title if he has one, according to his preference.

Envelope

Only on envelopes are the graded service titles used.

Brigadiers

In speech

Brigadiers are addressed by rank and surname, e.g. Brigadier Luttrell.

In writing

Letter

Formally

Formal manner of address in writing is Sir.

Socially

The social manner is Dear Brigadier Luttrell.

Envelope

Brigadier S. B. Luttrell

Colonels

In speech

Colonels are addressed by rank and surname, e.g. Colonel Howe.

In writing

Letter

Formally

The formal manner of address in writing is Sir.

Socially

The social manner, Dear Colonel Howe.

Envelope

Colonel F. E. Howe

Lieutenant-Colonels

In speech

Lieutenant-Colonels are addressed by rank and surname, e.g. Colonel Newcombe.

In writing

Letter

Formally

The formal manner of address in writing is Sir.

Socially

The social manner, Dear Colonel Newcombe.

Envelope

Only on envelopes is the graded title used. The regiment is added after the name, thus:

Lieut-Colonel H. Newcombe, RHA

Majors
Captains

In speech
Majors and Captains are addressed by name and rank, e.g. Major Shaw and Captain Shaw.

In writing   *Letter*

Formally   The formal manner of address in writing is Sir.

Socially   The social manner is Dear Major (or Captain) Shaw.

Envelope

Major (or Captain) E. Shaw, 11th Hussars

Lieutenants
Second-Lieutenants

In speech
Lieutenants are addressed as Mr.

In writing   *Letter*

Formally   The formal manner in writing is Sir.

Socially   The social manner, Dear Mr Fry.

Envelope

Official and   Lieut (*or* 2nd Lieut) T. W. Fry, 2nd Life Guards
Service

Socially   T. W. Fry, Esq., 2nd Life Guards

Medical Officers

Medical Officers should be addressed by rank, prefixed by the name of their branch when referred to.

Chaplains

In speech and writing
The Chaplain-General to the Forces ranks as major-general, and there are four classes below him, ranking respectively as colonels, lieutenant-colonels, majors, and captains. In no circumstances however, should military titles be used.

They are all addressed in speech and in writing according to their rank as clergymen. The Chaplain-General himself is an Archdeacon.

Envelope

To the Chaplain-General of the Forces

Other chaplains have the abbreviation CF or SCF added to their names.

Titled Officers

A hereditary or conferred title is preceded by the military one, as:

Examples Colonel Lord John Bull, 10th Lancers
             General Sir James Horn

Retired Officers

Retired officers do not have a regiment appended to their names. It used to be the practice for retired officers under the rank of Major to drop their title, but now a retired captain will be addressed by his rank if he chooses to use it.

Decorations

Abbreviations are shown immediately after the name, thus:

Examples Colonel Newcombe, VC
           T.W. Fry, Esq., MC, 2nd Life Guards

They should, of course, never be omitted.

Territorial Army

Usage is similar to that for professional members of the Army but forms of address should be employed only on army business.

THE ARMED FORCES:
Royal Air Force

The rules relating to the Navy and the Army apply in general. All service titles are used officially, but service titles below that of Flight Lieutenant are not used socially. Decorations and honours should never be omitted from envelopes. For ranks below Air Commodore the abbreviation RAF will be added after the name and any decorations and orders. Air Commodores and above are officially graded as 'air officers'.

Marshals of the Royal Air Force

They will normally be holders of some other title, and should be addressed accordingly.

In writing

Envelope

Marshal of the Royal Air Force Lord (*or* any other title) . . . . .

Air Chief Marshals
Air Marshals
Air Vice-Marshals

In speech

All are addressed as Air Marshal . . . . but the professional title is never further abbreviated.

In writing

Letter

Formally

The formal manner of address in writing is Sir.

Socially

The social manner in writing is Dear Air Marshal (*or* Air Marshal Smith), *or* by his title if he has one, according to his preference.

Envelope

Only on envelopes are graded service titles used.

Air Commodores

In speech
Air Commodores are addressed by rank and surname, e.g. Air Commodore Jones.

In writing
Letter
Formally
The formal manner of address is Sir.
Socially
The social manner is Dear Air Commodore Jones.

Envelope
Air Commodore G. H. Jones
The service title is never abbreviated in social usage.

Group Captains
Wing Commanders
Squadron Leaders

In speech
They may be referred to as The Group Captain, *or* Group Captain White *or* addressed as:

Squadron Leader *or* Squadron Leader Black

In writing
Letter
Formally
The formal manner of address is Sir.
Socially
The social manner is, e.g. Dear Wing Commander Thomson.

Envelope
Group Captain J. C. White, RAF
The service titles are never abbreviated in social usage.

Flight Lieutenants

In speech
Flight Lieutenants are referred to and addressed by rank and surname, e.g. Flight Lieutenant Brown, but not as Flight Lieutenant.

In writing

Letter

Formally and socially

The formal and social manner of writing is Flight Lieutenant Brown.

Envelope

Flight Lieutenant Brown

The service title is never abbreviated in social usage.

Flying Officers
Pilot Officers

In speech

The service titles are used only for official purposes. Social manner of address is Mr Gray.

In writing

Letter

Formally and socially

The formal manner of writing is Sir, the social manner is Dear Mr Gray.

Envelope

A. B. Gray, Esq., RAF

Medical Officers

Medical Officers should be addressed by rank, prefixed by the name of their branch when referred to.

Chaplains

The Chaplain-in-Chief, Royal Air Force, has the relative rank of Air Vice-Marshal, and other Royal Air Force chaplains have ranks relative to Group Captain down to Flight Lieutenant.

In speech

Chaplains are, however, known and addressed both officially and otherwise according to their ecclesiastical titles, which for the Chaplain-in-Chief is Archdeacon, and not by their relative status in the Royal Air Force.

In writing

Envelope

The Reverend A. Green, RAF, *not* Squadron Leader the Rev. A. Green.

Titled Officers

A hereditary or conferred title is preceded by the RAF one, as:

Examples Air Commodore Lord Robert Thomas
Squadron Leader Sir William Evans

Retired Officers

A retired officer who has the rank of Squadron Leader or above should be addressed in exactly the same way as one on the active list, except that the abbreviation 'Rtd' should be added whenever it is necessary to indicate the fact. For instance, a private letter should be addressed without the suffix, but a letter to a retired officer working, say in the Ministry of Defence should add 'Rtd'.

Decorations

Abbreviations are placed immediately after the name.

Examples Group Captain J. C. White, DSO, RAF
A. B. Gray, Esq., DFC, RAF

Royal Air Force Volunteer Reserve

Usage is similar to that for professional members of the Royal Air Force but forms of address should be employed only on RAF business.

THE ARMED FORCES:
Women's Services

The comparative ranks in Navy, Army and Air Force are given in the table on page 114.

Their use is, in general, the same as for men's service:

In speech

Officially or formally they are addressed by service rank or, by those junior, as Ma'am. Socially it is more usual to address them as, e.g. Mrs Barrett or Miss Barrett.

Officers with titles of their own are addressed by them unless they prefer to be addressed by rank.

In writing

Letter

Madam is used instead of Sir in more formal letters; service titles are never abbreviated; titled officers are addressed as such.

Envelope

Service titles are never abbreviated; the personal initials and name should be followed by decorations (if any) and the initials of the service:

WRNS, WRAC or WRAF

Example Wing Commander C. M. Barrett, WRAF

LAW, DIPLOMATIC AND GOVERNMENT

The various titles and offices are given alphabetically.

Agents-General

These are the representatives in London of the provincial or state government (not the Federal Governments) of Canada or Australia. They are addressed according to their own name and rank, with their office following the name on an envelope.

Aldermen

(This paragraph now applies only to Aldermen of the Corporation of London and in certain parts of Northern Ireland, since the office has been abolished elsewhere.)

In speech

During the term of office an alderman is addressed as Alderman or Madam Alderman.

In writing

Letter

Formally

Dear Sir, *or*
Dear Madam,

Socially

Dear Alderman, *or*
Dear Alderman Jones, *or*
Dear Madam Alderman,

Envelope

If an Alderman possesses another title this should of course be used; in such cases Alderman precedes

In writing	*Envelope* (continued)

other designations; Mr, Mrs or Miss, however, are used before the word Alderman.

Alderman Sir Joseph Jones
Mr Alderman J. Jones
Mrs Alderman Jones

Ambassadors

In speech	The formal and social manner of address in speech is Your Excellency or Sir *or* Madam.
In writing	*Letter*
Formally	My Lord *or* Lady (or Sir *or* Madam, according to rank),
	I have the honour to be, my Lord *or* Lady (or Sir *or* Madam), Your Excellency's obedient servant,
Socially	Dear Mr *or* Mrs, Miss Whitby (Sir Charles *or* Lady Jane, or according to rank), Yours sincerely,

Envelope

His Excellency Mr Charles Whitby, CMG (*not* Esq.)
or
His Excellency Sir Charles Whitby, KCMG
or
Her Excellency Mrs Jane Whitby

The form of address for the Apostolic Pro-nuncio is His Excellency, followed by clerical rank.

American ambassadors

The Honorable Charles Whitby
This title is retained for life.

Ambassadors' wives do not share their husbands' official title of Excellency, although it is still accorded them by courtesy in some countries, and the usage has not entirely ceased in others.

Ambassadors' husbands do not share the title of Excellency. They should be addressed according to their own rank or title.

Attorneys-General

In speech

Attorneys-General are addressed in speech according to their name and rank. They are invariably QCs and the rules as for Queen's Counsel apply.

In writing

In letters or on envelopes they may be addressed by name and rank or, on the latter, as The Attorney-General.

Bailies (of Scottish Burghs)

In speech

During their term of office they are addressed as Bailie.

In writing

Letter

Socially

Dear Bailie Campbell

Envelope

Bailie J. Campbell

Chairmen of County Councils

In speech

The Chairman of a County Council is addressed as Mr Chairman, even though the Chairman for the time being be a lady.

In writing

Envelope

The Chairman of . . . . County Council

Chairmen of District Councils

Since local government reorganisation cities and towns which once called their civic heads Lord Mayor or Mayor, Lord Provost or Provost in Scotland, have become districts, and their civic heads Chairmen of District Councils. Nevertheless, in those cities and towns which had Mayors or Provosts in the past the Chairman of the District Council may still be so described, and the forms of address shown under Lord Mayor, Lord Provost, Mayor and Provost still apply (*see* pages 144, 145, 148, 151). Otherwise they are addressed in the same way as Chairmen of County Councils.

Chargés d'affaires

Chargés d'affaires usually take the place temporarily of ambassadors at embassies and of ministers at legations, while at a few posts the office is a permanent one. They rank below envoys-extraordinary (*see* **Ministers** page 149) in diplomatic circles, but the same rules apply.

Circuit Judges

In speech
Formally and
socially

Circuit Judges are addressed and referred to on the Bench as Your Honour and His *or* Her Honour. Socially they are addressed and referred to in conversation as Judge or Judge Jones.

Where two judges have the same (or even a very similar) surname, the second to be appointed will choose to be known by one of his forenames as well as his surname; for example, Mr Henry Roberts Jones is made a Circuit Judge, and (because there is already a Judge, or a Mr Justice Jones) is known as His Honour Judge Roberts Jones.

In writing	*Letter*

Dear Judge, *or*
Dear Judge Jones,

Yours sincerely,

Envelope

His *or* Her Honour Judge Jones

Queen's Counsel who are appointed Circuit Judges continue to use the initials QC after their names.

Retired Circuit Judges

The title His/Her Honour is now retained after retirement, omitting the word Judge, and adding the forename or initials; so that the address of Judge Jones on the envelope is:

His Honour Henry Jones

Consuls

In speech   They are addressed according to name and rank.

In writing   *Letter*

They are addressed according to name and rank.

Envelope

Name should be followed by

HM Agent and Consul-General *or*
HM Consul-General *or*
HM Consul *or*
HM Vice-Consul

Conveners

The Chairman of a Regional or District Council in Scotland is often known as the Convener or Convenor (both spellings are used).

He (or she) is addressed in the same way as for a Chairman, except that in speech he (or she) is called Convener, without the 'Mr', 'Mrs' or 'Miss'.

Councillors

In speech   During the term of office the manner of address is
                   Councillor.

In writing   *Letter*
Formally   Dear Sir *or* Madam,
Socially   Dear Councillor, *or*
                   Dear Councillor Peters,

                   Envelope
                   Councillor S. Peters

                   If a Councillor possesses another title this should be
                   used; in such cases Councillor precedes other
                   designations, including Mrs or Miss.

                   Councillor Sir Stanley Peters
                   Councillor Mrs Peters

                   It is better not to add the title Councillor to other
                   titles unless writing on Council business.

Deputy Lieutenants of Counties

In speech and Deputy Lieutenants are addressed according to their
writing   name and rank. For official letters the affix DL
                   should be used (*see* page163).

District Judges (Magistrates' Courts)

The same rules are followed as for **Justices of the
Peace** (*see* page 141), except that the letters JP are
not used for District Judges.

Envoys-Extraordinary
Ministers-Plenipotentiary

See under **Ministers (Diplomatic Service)**, page
149.

Governors-General
Governors
Lieutenant-Governors

In speech

Governors-General and Governors are addressed as 'His *or* Her Excellency' while holding office; the wives of Governors-General are also so addressed, but not the wives of Governors. (Husbands should be addressed according to rank and title.) The Lieutenant-Governors of Jersey, Guernsey, the Isle of Man and Canadian provinces have the same style. For states in Australia see below.

In writing

The Governor-General of Canada is called 'Right Honourable' for life. The wife or husband is called 'Her *or* His Excellency'. The Lieutenant-Governors of Canadian provinces (there are no Governors) are called 'The Honourable' for life, whereas the deputy of the Governor of an Australian state, who is also known as Lieutenant-Governor, is not addressed as 'His *or* Her Excellency' – or referred to as 'The Honourable' unless already so styled.

Formally

Sir *or* Madam

I have the honour to be, Sir *or* Madam,
Your Excellency's obedient servant,

Socially

Dear Governor-General/Governor/Lieutenant-Governor,

Yours sincerely,

Envelope

Her Excellency the Governor-General of . . . .
His Excellency, the Right Hon. Sir John . . . . ,
    Governor-General of Canada
Her Excellency Mrs Christine . . . . , Governor of
    . . . .
His Excellency Mr J. H. . . . . . , Governor and
    Commander-in-Chief of (Jersey or Guernsey).

HM Lord-Lieutenants of Counties

(*See* **Lord-Lieutenants of Counties**)

High Commissioners

In speech

High Commissioners represent their country of the Commonwealth in another country. They are in effect Ambassadors, and are addressed similarly (*see* page 132).

In writing   *Letter*

Formally

Your Excellency,

I have the honour to be
Your Excellency's obedient servant,

Socially

Dear High Commissioner,

Believe me
Dear High Commissioner,
Yours sincerely,

Envelope

His *or* Her Excellency to precede
    Mr, Mrs or Miss . . . . .
    The Honourable . . . . .
    The Right Honourable . . . . .
    (according to rank)

Honourable

The title 'Honourable' is accorded in the Commonwealth and other English-speaking countries to holders of a number of public offices, including Ministers (or their equivalent), Judges, members of *some* legislative bodies, Governors or Lieutenant-Governors, and so on. It may be held for life or during tenure of office; within the scope of this book it is sufficient to say that the usage exists and should be followed where it appears; and that it is not usual to abbreviate 'The Honorable' in the United States.

Judges of the High Court

MEN

High Court Judges are usually knighted on appointment.

In speech

They are addressed and referred to as My Lord and Your (or His) Lordship on the Bench, in the precincts of the Court, and whenever they are being approached in their judicial capacity.

In their private capacities they may be addressed in speech as 'Mr Justice Smith', as 'Judge', or as 'Sir John'.

In writing

Letter

Formally

According to circumstances:

My Lord, *or*
Sir,

Socially

Address by rank.

Envelope

The Hon. Mr Justice Swift (to a court address) *or*
The Hon. Sir John Swift (to a private address)

WOMEN

In 1965 the first woman Judge of the High Court was appointed, and there are now a number. They are made Dame of the Most Excellent Order of the British Empire on their appointment.

In speech

Judges are addressed in Court as My Lady and Your (*or* Her) Ladyship. Socially they may be addressed as:

Mrs Justice . . . . . *or*
Dame . . . . .

The style 'Mrs Justice' is used by unmarried judges also.

In writing

Envelope

The Hon. Dame . . . . , DBE *or*
The Hon. Mrs Justice . . . . , DBE

As with **Circuit Judges** (*see* page 134), the second to be appointed of two High Court Judges with the same name will have chosen to be known by a forename in addition.

Queen's Counsel who are appointed High Court Judges no longer use the initials QC after their name.

Presidents of the Three High Court Divisions

The High Court has three divisions, Chancery, Queen's Bench, and Family Divisions, and each division has a President.

The Lord High Chancellor of Great Britain is by virtue of his office President of the Chancery Division, and the judge who normally acts for him in that capacity is known as the Vice-Chancellor; the Lord Chief Justice of England is President of the Queen's Bench Division; and one of the judges of the Family Division is appointed its President.

These judges are not addressed as Hon. Mr Justice; the Lord Chancellor and Lord Chief Justice are addressed as such (*see* page 143), and the other two by their names and offices, or by their offices alone.

In writing

Envelope

The Hon. Sir Charles Brown, The Vice-Chancellor
or
The Vice-Chancellor
and
The Right Hon. Sir Maurice Smith,
  President of the Family Division
or
The President of the Family Division

(Hon. or Right Hon. depending on whether the judge is a Privy Counsellor.)

Retired Judges of the High Court

After retirement, the address on the envelope is:

The Hon. Sir John Swift

Judges overseas

Judges of the High Courts or Supreme Courts of Commonwealth countries or overseas territories are addressed during office as:

The Honourable the Chief Justice, *or*
The Hon. Mr or Mrs Justice . . . .

In Australia, Judges of the High Court are now addressed as The Hon. Justice . . . . .
The Chief Justice of Canada bears the title 'The Right Honourable' for life. Other Judges of Commonwealth countries may be Privy Counsellors, when they will be addressed as Right Hon. also. It is not unusual in some countries for a Judge who has held office for some time to be granted the title 'The Honourable' for life. Otherwise no special form of address is used on retirement.

Justices of the Peace

In speech

Justices of the Peace are addressed on the Bench as Your Worship.

In writing

Envelope

Formally

When writing to a Justice of the Peace in his or her official capacity (and only then), the affix JP should be used (*see* page 163).

Socially

As an **Esquire** (see page 74), or according to rank.

Lady Mayoresses

Rules as for wives of **Lord Mayors** apply (*see* page 144).

Law Lords

(*See* **Life Peers**, page 6.)

Lord-Lieutenants and Lieutenants of Counties

In speech

Lord-Lieutenants are addressed according to their rank.

In writing

Envelope

His Grace the Duke of Middlesex, KG,
    HM Lord-Lieutenant for . . . . .

If a commoner, the form is:

Alan Smith, Esq., HM Lord-Lieutenant for . . . .
or
Mrs Angela Smith, HM Lord-Lieutenant for . . . .

At the time of the amalgamation of some counties under the Local Government Act 1972, the appointment formerly known as HM Lieutenant (commonly called Lord-Lieutenant), became officially HM Lord-Lieutenant; and some additional appointments were made, so that a new county consisting of two or more formerly separate counties might have a Lord-Lieutenant and one or two Lieutenants. The appointment of a Lieutenant was only made when the new county included two counties each of which had previously had its own Lord-Lieutenant.

A Lieutenant is also addressed according to his *or* her rank, with the addition of the appointment:

Colonel J. S. Napier, DSO, HM Lieutenant for

. . . .

Lord Advocate of Scotland

In speech
Formally and
socially

Formerly addressed as My Lord, etc., but now, probably from ceasing to be on the Bench, more frequently as Sir. He is socially addressed as Lord Advocate.

He may be a member of the House of Lords or of the House of Commons, but need not be either; he is always a Privy Counsellor.

In writing	*Letter* Dear Lord Advocate,
	Envelope The Right Hon the Lord Advocate

Lord of Appeal in Ordinary

Rules as for **Barons and Baronesses** (*see* page 45) apply also to the Lord of Appeal, husband or wife, and children.

Lord Chamberlain

The Lord Chamberlain is addressed according to rank and title.

Lord Chancellor

In speech	The Lord Chancellor is addressed as Lord Chancellor, and referred to in speech and writing either by his appointment or according to his rank in the peerage.
In writing Formally	*Envelope* The Right Hon. the Lord Chancellor *or* (in the most formal circumstances) The Right Hon. the Lord High Chancellor of Great Britain

Lord Chief Justice

In speech	The Lord Chief Justice is a peer, and is addressed and referred to accordingly.

In writing	*Letter*
Socially	A social letter may begin:
	Dear Lord Chief Justice,
Formally and socially	*Envelope*
	The Right Hon. the Lord Chief Justice of England

Lord Justice of Appeal

A Lord Justice of Appeal will already be a High Court Judge and therefore a knight or a dame.

In speech   A Lord Justice of Appeal, is addressed and referred to as My Lord *or* My Lady and His Lordship *or* Her Ladyship.

In writing   *Letter*

They are addressed by professional, semi-professional and semi-official correspondents as:

Dear Lord *or* Lady Justice,

In writing   *Envelope*

The Right Hon. Lord *or* Lady Justice . . . .
or, privately,
The Right Hon. Sir Henry . . . . .
The Right Hon. Dame Elizabeth . . . . .

Lord of the Manor

Such a lordship confers no rank or title.

Lord Mayors

The Lord Mayors of Belfast, Cardiff, Dublin, London and York, and of the Australian cities of Adelaide, Brisbane, Hobart, Melbourne, Sydney, and Perth are entitled to the style Right Hon. while they are in office. This is, however, only an official and not a personal prefix, and it is used only with the title 'Lord Mayor' and not with the Lord Mayor's own name; it is incorrect to address such a Lord Mayor as, for example, 'The Right Hon. Richard Whittington'. The form of address does not vary when the Lord Mayor is a woman.

In speech

The formal mode of address is My Lord, while socially they are addressed according to their own name and rank.

In writing

Letter

The formal mode of address is My Lord, while socially they are addressed according to their own name and rank.

Envelope

The Right Hon. the Lord Mayor of . . . . .

The Mayors of certain other cities also are designated 'Lord Mayors', and are addressed according to these rules, except as to the envelope which should be addressed

The Right Worshipful the Lord Mayor of . . . . .

Lady Mayoresses (women)

The formal mode of address for a woman acting as Lady Mayoress is, both in speech and writing, My Lady. Lady Mayoresses do not share the honour of the style Right Hon.

In writing

Envelope

The Lady Mayoress of . . . . .

(men)

Where a man has the role of Lord Mayor's escort, it is best to ascertain his particular wishes. It is likely that he will wish to be addressed according to his own name and rank.

Lord Privy Seal

The Lord Privy Seal is addressed according to his own name and title.

Lord Provosts

Under the Local Government (Scotland) Act, 1973, the title of Lord Provost attaches to the Chairmen of the District Councils of Dundee, Aberdeen, Edinburgh and Glasgow.

The Lord Provost of Edinburgh and the Lord Provost of Glasgow should both be addressed as 'The Right Hon. the Lord Provost of . . . .'; 'The Right Hon.' should not be used in front of their names.

In speech

During office Lord Provosts are addressed and referred to as My Lord and His Lordship. The Lord Provost of Glasgow is referred to socially as 'The Lord Provost' and addressed as Lord Provost (not, except in historical comparison, Lord Provost Campbell).

In writing

Letter

Dear Lord Provost,

Envelope

The Right Hon. the Lord Provost of Edinburgh (*or* Glasgow)
The Lord Provost of . . . . .

Wives

Wives do not share the title, though there has been a tendency to refer to them as The Lady Provost, which has led to such incorrect descriptions as 'Lord Provost Campbell and the Lady Provost of . . . . ', which should be avoided.

Lords of Session

A Lord of Session is a Judge of the Court of Session (or Senator of the Court of Justice) of Scotland who, upon elevation to the Bench, is styled for life The Hon. Lord *or* Lady, with surname or a territorial name according to choice. This is a title of judicial office, and not a peerage.

If a Lord of Session is also a Privy Counsellor he *or* she is, or course, addressed as The Right Hon. Lord *or* Lady . . . . .

In speech

They are addressed as My Lord *or* My Lady.

In writing

Letter

Dear Lord . . . . . ,

Envelope

The Hon. Lord . . . . .

The Lord Justice-General and the Lord Justice-Clerk of Scotland are Lords of Session and Privy Counsellors. They are always addressed by their office:

The Right Hon. the Lord Justice-General
The Right Hon. the Lord Justice-Clerk

Upon giving up this office they revert to the style of a Lord of Session who is a Privy Counsellor.

Wives and Husbands

Wives are addressed in writing as Lady . . . . , and in other respects as the wife of a Baron (*see* page 45), but without the prefix 'The Right Hon.' or 'The'. Husbands are addressed according to their own rank or office. Children have no title.

Magistrates

See under **Justices of the Peace** (page 141) and **District Judges (Magistrates' Courts)** (page 136).

Master of the Rolls

Rules as for **Judges** apply (*see* page 139).

In writing

Envelope

The Right Hon. The Master of the Rolls *or*
The Right Hon. (according to rank)

Masters of the Supreme Court

Masters of the Supreme Court are addressed
according to own name and rank, except in court,
when they are addressed and referred to as, e.g.
Master Robson.

Mayors

The Mayors of certain cities use the description
'Lord Mayor' (*see* page 144 under that heading).

In speech

Male Mayors are addressed as an Esquire (*see* page
74), *or* according to own rank.

Women are addressed as 'Your Worship' *or* 'Mr
Mayor'; colloquially 'Madam Mayor' is sometimes
used, but this is not an established mode of address.

In writing

Mayors are addressed according to their own rank.

Envelope

Mayor of a city
Mayor of a
borough

The Right Worshipful the Mayor of . . . . .
The Worshipful the Mayor of . . . .

Mayoresses

In speech

Mayoresses are addressed as 'Mayoress', never
'Your Worship', or 'Mr Mayor'. If a Mayoress is a
Justice of the Peace and is sitting on the Bench, then
the term 'Your Worship' would, of course, be used
when addressing the Bench.

In writing

Mayoresses are addressed according to their own rank.

Members of Parliament

According to rank, with MP after the name.

There is no established convention for the use of postnominals in the case of Members of the European Parliament, of the Scottish Parliament, of the National Assembly for Wales, of the Northern Ireland Assembly and of the House of Keys, Isle of Man.

Ministers (Government)

All cabinet ministers in the UK are Privy Counsellors and Members of Parliament (House of Commons or House of Lords). Otherwise they are addressed according to their own rank or title.

Ministers (Diplomatic Service)

In speech and writing

The title Envoy-Extraordinary and Minister-Plenipotentiary, given to the head of a Legation, was customarily abbreviated to Minister. Now all posts have been elevated to Ambassador, and all Legations to Embassy.

Ministers, Ministers (Economic), or Ministers (Commercial), may serve under the Ambassador in a large Embassy; but their title merely indicates their diplomatic service rank and they are not given any special form of address, as they would be if they were Ministers Plenipotentiary at the head of a Legation.

Police

For reasons of security, omit rank and occupation from any envelope sent to a home address.

Metropolitan and City of London Police

Commissioner
Deputy or Assistant Commissioner

Other Police Forces

Chief Constable
Deputy or Assistant Chief Constable

In speech   Men or women of these ranks are addressed by name or by appointment.

In writing   *Letter*

Formally   Dear Sir,
Dear Madam,

Socially   Dear Mr (or Mrs, or Miss) Dixon, *or*
Dear Chief Constable

Envelope

The envelope is addressed with the name, followed by appointment and Force.

Sir George Dixon, CBE
Commissioner of Police of the Metropolis

George Dixon, Esq., OBE
Deputy Chief Constable, ... Constabulary

Commanders
Chief Superintendents
Superintendents

In speech   Men or women of these ranks may be addressed either with the rank before the name or with Mr, Mrs, or Miss.

In writing   *Letter*

Same rules as above.

In writing

Envelope

Superintendent G. Dixon
. . . . . . Constabulary
G. Dixon, Esq., QPM
Chief Superintendent, Metropolitan Police

Other Ranks

Below the ranks described above, the rank is always used before the name.

On envelopes the Force follows the name.

Presidents

Presidents of foreign countries should be addressed as Your Excellency and referred to as His/Her Excellency. The US president, however, should be addressed as Mr President and on envelopes as the President of the United States of America.

Prime Ministers

In the United Kingdom Prime Ministers are always Privy Counsellors and are so addressed, according to rank.

The Prime Ministers of many Commonwealth countries are also members of the Privy Council. If they are not Privy Counsellors, they are customarily addressed as Hon. during the period of office.

Right Hon. for life by virtue of his office, whether or not a Privy Counsellor.

Provosts of Scottish Cities

Rules apply as in the case of an **Esquire** (*see* page 74) but a Provost will be referred to locally as The Provost, rather than 'Mr *or* Mrs' . . . . .

The Civic Heads of Edinburgh, Dundee, Aberdeen, and Glasgow are known as Lord Provost (*see* page 146).

Queen's Counsel

They should be addressed according to rank, with the initials QC appended to the name on envelopes.

When a Queen's Counsel is appointed a Circuit Judge, he or she continues to use the initials, but Judges of the High Court cease to use them.

Recorders

Recorders are barristers or solicitors. They should be addressed as an Esquire (*see* page 74), or according to rank.

On the bench they are addressed as 'Your Honour'.

The Recorders may be Queen's Counsel, in which case the initials QC should be added on envelopes.

Sheriffs

England, Wales and Northern Ireland

Sheriffs are appointed in all counties and in some cities, including the City of London, as officials of the Crown historically concerned with the administration of justice.

Sheriffs of counties are known as High Sheriffs, indicating that theirs is a senior appointment.

In speech

They may be addressed on formal occasions as High Sheriff (of counties), or Sheriff or Mr *or* Mrs Sheriff (of cities).

In writing

Letter

The office of Sheriff requires no special form of address. Rules apply as in the case of an Esquire (*see* page 74), or according to rank.

In writing	*Envelope*
Official business	Colonel J. C. W. Browne, DSO
	High Sheriff of . . . . shire

Scotland

Sheriffs are Judges of the Sheriff Courts. There are six Sheriffs-Principal, and within each of their jurisdictions a number of Sheriffs.

In speech	
In court	My Lord *or* My Lady (whether Sheriff-Principal or Sheriff)
Officially and socially	Sheriff . . . . . (whether Sheriff-Principal or Sheriff)

The Sheriff-Principal is announced and referred to as the Sheriff-Principal of . . . . . *(see below, under envelope)*.

In writing   *Letter*

The office requires no special form of address. Rules apply as in the case of an **Esquire** *(see* page 74), *or* according to rank.

Envelope

Rules apply as follows:

Part-time:	Esq. (or according to rank)
Full-time:	Sheriff Robert Mackenzie

The Sheriff-Principal is, however, addressed as:

William Douglas, Esq. (or according to rank), Sheriff-Principal of . . . . .

using the first territorial name of conjoined shrievalties (areas of jurisdiction).

Stipendiary Magistrates

Now District Judges (Magistrates' Courts): *see* page
136.

Vice Lord-Lieutenants

They are addressed according to name and rank. The
abbreviation VL following the name is not used.

THE UNIVERSITIES

Chancellors

In speech

Chancellors are addressed formally as Sir *or*, Madam, or according to rank. More familiarly as Mr Chancellor or Chancellor.

In writing   *Letter*

Formally

Sir *or* Madam (or according to rank),
I am, Sir *or* Madam,
Your obedient servant,

Less formally

Dear Sir *or* Madam,
Yours faithfully,

Socially

Dear Chancellor,
Yours sincerely,

Envelope

John Mansfield, Esq.
   Chancellor of the University of . . . . *or*
The Right Hon. the Earl of . . . . .
   Chancellor of the University of . . . . .

Vice-Chancellors

In speech

The rules as for Chancellors apply. The prefix is used only with the office, not with the individual's name.

In writing   *Letter*

Formally

The rules as for Chancellors apply.

In writing

Socially

Dear Vice-Chancellor,

Yours sincerely,

Envelope

The Vice-Chancellor of The University of . . . . .

The two exceptions to this are Vice-Chancellors of Oxford and Cambridge, who are addressed respectively as:

The Rev. the Vice-Chancellor of The University of Oxford (whether or not the Vice-Chancellor is in Holy Orders) *and*
The Right Worshipful the Vice-Chancellor of The University of Cambridge

High Stewards

In speech

High Stewards are appointed in the Universities of Oxford and Cambridge. They are addressed according to their rank.

In writing

Letter

Formally

Sir (or according to rank),

I am, Sir,
Your obedient servant,

Less formally

Dear Sir,

Yours faithfully,

Socially

Dear High Steward,

Yours sincerely,

Envelope

His Grace the Duke of . . . . .
    High Steward of The University of . . . . .

Deputy High Stewards

Rules apply as for High Stewards.

Heads of Colleges

They may be known as Masters, Mistresses, Presidents, Principals, Provosts, Rectors, or Wardens.

In speech   They are addressed formally as Sir or Madam. Socially by name and rank.

In writing   *Letter*

Formally   Sir *or* Madam (or according to rank),
Your obedient servant,

Less formally   Dear Sir *or* Madam (or according to rank),
Yours faithfully,

Socially   Dear Master *or* Mistress (or according to college title),
Yours sincerely,

Envelope

The Master (*or* according to college title) of . . . . College

Deans

Deans of colleges are addressed according to their own name and rank. In the rare cases (cathedral colleges) where a dean is head he will also be a dean of the Church of England and must be addressed as such (*see* page 87).

Principals in Scotland and Wales

The head of a Scottish University may be appointed Principal and Vice-Chancellor, and the heads of the Constituent Colleges of the University of Wales are known as Principals.

The same rules of address apply as for **Heads of Colleges**.

Professors

In speech	The title is used both formally and socially.
In writing	*Letter*
Formally	Dear Sir (*or* Madam), I am, dear Sir (*or* Madam), Your obedient servant,
Less formally	Dear Sir (*or* Madam), Yours faithfully,
Socially	Dear Professor Dash, Yours sincerely,
	Envelope Professor J. G. Dash

Ordained Professors

In speech	An ordained professor is referred and spoken to as a Professor.
In writing	*Letter* As for a Professor.
	Envelope The Rev. Professor W. L. Fleetwood

If Canon, he *or* she is addressed as such (*see* page 90). Such accumulations as Professor the Rev. Canon . . . , though not unknown, are undesirable.

Doctors

Degrees are given by the older and most of the newer universities in seven faculties: Divinity, Law, Literature, Medicine, Music, Philosophy and Science. The following are the various styles and abbreviations:

Doctor of Divinity   DD
Doctor of Laws   LLD

Conferred by Cambridge and all other universities granting degrees in this faculty.

Doctor of Civil Law   DCL

This is the Oxford, Durham and Newcastle upon Tyne degree corresponding to the Cambridge LLD.

Doctor of Literature ⎫ Doctors of Letters ⎭	LittD	Cambridge, Dublin and Liverpool)
	DLitt	(Oxford and some others)
	DLit	(London and Manchester)
Doctor of Medicine	MD	(all universities except Oxford)
	DM	(Oxford)
Doctor of Music	MusD	(Cambridge and Durham)
	DMus	(Oxford)
Doctor of Philosophy	PhD	(Cambridge and others)
	DPhil	(Oxford)
Doctor of Science	ScD	(Cambridge and Dublin)
	DSc	(Oxford and others)

In writing

Letter

Rules as for Esquires, with Dr substituted for Mr, Mrs or Miss.

Envelope

It is a matter of individual choice whether the holder of a doctorate is addressed as Dr . . . . . or as John . . . . . , Esq., with the appropriate lettering, except that it is now the custom always to write the letters DD (*See also* **Doctors of Medicine**, *below*)

It is never correct to write Dr . . . . . , PhD (or whatever the lettering may be).

Outside academic circles even doctorates would not be appended to the name in social letters, although of course, anyone customarily known as Dr . . . . . would still be so.

Doctors of Divinity

Doctors of Divinity are usually but not always clergymen. The degree can, in some universities, be taken by, or conferred on, laymen as well.

In speech

In the case of the clergy, they are addressed and referred to as Dr Read.

In writing

Letter

Formally

Reverend Sir,

Yours faithfully,

Socially

Dear Dr Read,

Yours sincerely,

Envelope

The Rev. J. L. Read, DD

Doctors of Medicine

The title has become so wedded to the medical profession that the reminder is needed that not all qualified medical men hold the final degree.

Those who hold the final degree are addressed and referred to as Dr Gray. Those medical men who have not taken the final degree are addressed as if they have. There is also the firmly established custom in the medical profession of addressing surgeons as Esquires. Gynaecologists tend to be addressed as surgeons in England and Wales, as doctors elsewhere.

If a knighthood, baronetcy or peerage has been conferred, the address is according to rank.

In speech	Specialists and general practitioners are addressed as Dr, surgeons as Mr, Mrs or Miss unless the doctor has a rank above Esquire in which case rules for the particular rank will apply.
In writing	*Letter*
	According to rank. It is normal, however, to address general practitioners as Dr.
	Envelope
	Fully qualified doctors:

Thomas Gray, Esq., MD (but in Scotland, usually, Dr Thomas Gray)
Sir Thomas Gray, MD
Sir Thomas Gray, Bt, MD
The Right Hon. Lord Gray, MD

Doctors without final degrees take the letters relating to their qualification, e.g. MB, LRCP.
It is normal to address general practitioners simply as Dr Thomas Gray, without letters.

Surgeons:

Thomas Gray, Esq., FRCS *etc.*

Honorary Doctorates

The same rules apply as to other holders, although it is not usual to add letters after the name if there are other letters already. They may appear in the most comprehensive lists but they are not used in circumstances where they may seem to imply an academic qualification. Many holders of honorary doctorates do enjoy the use of the title Doctor, and their preference should be followed.

Lesser Degrees

The custom established and used by the older universities is really the best to follow. The rule is that doctors in any faculty use the designation (*see* **Doctors**), while lesser degrees are omitted.

Letters denoting masters' and bachelors' degrees, which are, of course, most common, are not used even in university circles in ordinary correspondence, and socially they are not used at all. There are certain formal occasions on which members of learned professions would use them, such as in lists of lectures, etc., but a master's or bachelor's degree would not be appended to a doctor's. The reason for this is that in the older universities a doctor's degree is considered to include an MA – it can only very rarely be taken without it.

Only the higher of two degrees in the same faculty would be used.

Master of Arts	MA
Bachelor of Arts	BA
Bachelor of Letters	BLitt
Bachelor of Divinity	BD
Master of Laws	LLM
Bachelor of Laws	LLB
Bachelor of Civil Law	BCL
Bachelor of Medicine	MB
Bachelor of Medicine	BM (Oxford)
Bachelor of Music	BMus MusB MusBac
Bachelor of Science	BSc

HONOURS, QUALIFICATIONS AND APPOINTMENTS

Notes on the Use of Abbreviations for Honorific and Other Affixes

In no circumstances do honorific initials (even VC) appear on visiting cards.

Honorific affixes, whether military decorations or not, should be appended in addressing formal letters; but not in the case of Privy Counsellors.

Affixes indicating professional qualification or official status should be used only when addressing the correspondent in his or her professional or official capacity. This includes DL and JP.

The order of letters after the name (and after the abbreviations Bt or Esq., if they apply) is fixed, and should be followed as set out below.

First

Decorations and Honours

These should not be omitted, if any letters are used at all, and in most cases it is preferable to include them in an address. They should be written in the sequence given on page 165.

Second

Appointments made by or on behalf of the Queen

If for any reason it is necessary to include the initials PC, they will come first, followed by ADC, QHP, QHS, QHDS, QHNS, QHC, QC, JP, DL. It should be noted, however, that PC is nowadays never used on envelopes, and that the next appointments (up to QHC) being short-term ones, are not normally used in ordinary correspondence, although they may be in official letters.

QC must always be used. JP and DL are used when writing on business connected with the appointment.

Third	**University Degrees**
	See pages 159–62.
Fourth	**Medical Qualifications Other than University Degrees**

In normal correspondence only those indicating fellowships or memberships are used. Medical precede surgical and are followed by more specialised fellowships. FRCP and FRCS should always appear (in that order) if held, and so should fellowships or memberships of other institutions that confer postgraduate qualifications.

Fifth　**Fellowships or Memberships of Learned Societies, Academies or Professional Institutions**

As a general rule, letters should be shown in the order of the foundation of the societies, etc., and no distinction is made, in the sequence, between fellowships and memberships. Where, however, a professional institution has fellows and members, only letters for the higher rank would be shown on any but professional correspondence.

Those fellowships, etc., election to which is a distinction should be used on all correspondence: FRS, RA or FRA, RSA, FBA are examples.

Initials which indicate merely that the fellow or member declares his interest in and support for the body concerned are used when the subject of his or her interest is the matter of the correspondence. Initials are also used to indicate professional eminence or qualification when writing on professional matters.

The members of the sixteen bodies which make up the Council of Engineering Institutions are chartered engineers; they are entitled to use the letters CEng, which are placed immediately before the first fellowship or membership that gives the right to use such initials:

J. B. MacTavish, Esq., CEng, MICE, FIMechE.

Similarly, fellows and members of the Royal Society of Chemistry are entitled to use the abbreviation CChem before the letters FRSC and MRSC.

Sixth

Appointments or Offices

These include such initials as MP, MLA, MLC, CC, WS.

Sequence of Decorations and Honours

The following list shows the correct sequence of the various degrees of Honours and Decorations of which the abbreviations are most commonly employed. A higher rank in an Order includes the lower, i.e. it is never correct to put GCB, KCB, or KCMG, CMG. All decorations and honours should be given.

For the sequence of letters after the name other than decorations and honours, *see* pages 163–5.

For the various orders of Knighthood, *see* pages 54–64.

For the explanation of abbreviations, *see* preliminary pages of this book.

VC, GC, KG/LG, KT/LT, KP, GCB, OM, GCSI, GCMG, GCIE, CI, GCVO, GBE, CH, KCB/DCB, KCSI, KCMG/DCMG, KCIE, KCVO/DCVO, KBE/DBE, CB, CSI, CMG, CIE, CVO, CBE, DSO, LVO, OBE, ISO, MVO, MBE, RRC, DSC, MC, DFC, AFC, ARRC, AM, DCM, CGM, GM, DSM, MM, DFM, AFM, QGM, BEM, QPM, SGM, VD, ERD, TD, ED, RD, VRD, AE.

Victoria Cross

The Victoria Cross is the most distinquished of all decorations, and is conferred for valour in all branches of the fighting services. Since 1920 it has been extended to include women. The abbreviation VC takes precedence of all other decorations and honours.

Other service decorations may be used in accordance with the list on page 165 in addressing a recipient in writing.

George Cross

The George Cross is awarded for acts of great heroism or of conspicuous courage in extreme danger. It is intended primarily for civilians (both men and women), but awards are also made to members of the fighting services in actions for which military honours are not normally granted. The abbreviation GC follows VC but takes precedence of all other decorations and honours.

Order of Merit – OM

A very distinguished order, limited to twenty-four members, ranking in precedence immediately after Knights Grand Cross of the Order of the Bath.

Order of the Companions of Honour – CH

An order limited to sixty-five members, for which women are equally eligible with men. It carries no titles, but holders use the initials CH after the name. It ranks in precedence after the 1st degree of the Order of the British Empire (GBE).

Commonwealth Countries

Many Commonwealth countries are instituting their own orders which are awarded to their own citizens and which are indicated (in the British fashion) by postnominal lettering.

Such orders may be conferred on citizens of other countries within the Commonwealth who have in some way served the country awarding the honour. It is customary to use the letters or distinguishing titles of such orders while in the country that conferred them, but not elsewhere.

For awards in all Commonweath countries, information can be obtained from the office of the Governor General or equivalent head of state, or on the website www.medals.co.uk

Antigua and Barbuda

Knight of the Most Excellent Order of the National Hero – KNH

The Most Distinguished Order of the Nation has three classes:

Knight Grand Collar – KGN
Knight Grand Cross – KGCN
Knight (or Dame) Commander – KCN/DCN

Australia

The Order of Australia has four grades:

Knight (or Dame) of the Order of Australia – AK, AD
Companion of the Order of Australia – AC
Officer of the Order of Australia – AO
Member of the Order of Australia – AM

These letters follow respectively OM, GBE, KBE and DSO.

Barbados

The Order of Barbados has four classes:

Knight (or Dame) of St Andrew – KA, DA
    whose letters follow CH
Companion of Honour of Barbados – CHB
The Crown of Merit, which is in two grades:
    The Gold Crown of Merit – GCM
    The Silver Crown of Merit – SCM
The Barbados Service Award, which is in two grades:
    The Barbados Service Star – BSS
    The Barbados Service Medal – BSM

Canada

The Order of Canada confers three honours:

Companion of the Order of Canada – CC
Officer of the Order of Canada – OC
Member of the Order of Canada – CM

The Order of Military Merit has three grades:

Commander of the Order – CMM
Officer of the Order – OMM
Member of the Order – MMM

VC or GC would precede any of these letters.

Following letters for the Order of Canada and the Order of Military Merit come letters for Canadian provincial orders:

Ordre national du Québec – GOQ, OQ, CQ
The Saskatchewan Order of Merit – SOM
The Order of Ontario – OOnt
The Order of British Columbia – OBC
Alberta Order of Excellence – AOE

Jamaica

The Order of Jamaica (member) – OJ
Letters entitle bearer to title 'Hon.'

New Zealand

The Order of New Zealand (member) – ONZ
  whose letters follow OM

The New Zealand Order of Merit has five grades
  whose letters follow ONZ:

Knight (or Dame) Grand Companion – GNZM
Knight (or Dame) – KNZM, DNZM
Companion – CNZM
Officer – ONZM
Member – MNZM

The Queen's Service Order of New Zealand – the letters QSO precede OBE, and QSM (Queen's Service Medal) follow QGM.

REPLYING FORMALLY TO FORMAL INVITATIONS

Royal invitations from the Queen

Invitations are sent by a member of the Queen's household:

The Lord Chamberlain

or The Lord Steward of the Household

or The Master of the Household

and replies should be addressed to the official who has sent the invitation.

Those who have received the invitation should reply formally, giving their name in the same form that appears on the invitation itself, viz

Mr and Mrs Albert Green

Hon. and Mrs Albert Green

Rev. and Mrs Albert Green

Hence: Mr and Mrs Albert Green present their compliments to

the Lord Chamberlain,

or the Lord Steward of the Household,

or the Master of the Household,

and then, either: and have the honour to obey Her Majesty's Command to

e.g. the state banquet on 9 November at 8 p.m.

the garden party on 14 June at 3 p.m.

luncheon on 23 March at 1 p.m.

or and much regret that they will be unable to obey Her Majesty's Command to . . . . on . . . . , owing to the illness of Mrs Albert Green. (The reason should be specific and adequate – a minor engagement would not be considered sufficient reason not to obey the Command.)

Royal invitations from other members of the Royal Family

The procedures follow a similar pattern, but the invitations are no longer commands, so the reply should be worded

Mr and Mrs Albert Green present their compliments to (the person who has sent the invitation)

and have much pleasure in accepting the invitation from (e.g.) HRH The Prince of Wales to the luncheon on 23 March at 1 p.m.

or   . . . . and much regret that they are unable to accept the invitation from His Royal Highness owing to . . . .

Invitations to official functions

Invitations are often accompanied by a printed reply card. This should always be used and rules out the need for other reply.

Where there is no such card, write a letter (with the address at the head):

Mr and Mrs Albert Green thank (e.g.) the Chairman and Council of the National Association of . . . . for their kind invitation for Friday, 15 October, which they accept with much pleasure.

or   . . . . which they much regret being unable to accept.

(Here, another engagement could be adequate reason if a reason is given.)

Invitations to private functions (including weddings)

Invitations are frequently addressed to, say, Mr/Mrs/Miss Evelyn Jones *and partner*, or *and family*. In a reply accepting the invitation, the names of those who will attend should be given.

Write a letter (with the address at the head) similar to that for official functions, but it should be written (and the envelope addressed) to the hostess only, even where the invitation comes from host and hostess.

In the case of weddings and similar social functions, there is an increasing tendency to reply informally, in which case the above recommendations do not apply.

Some Pronunciations of Proper Names

a	as in cat	ō	as in home
ah	as in father	o	as in dog
ay	as in day	ōō	as in food
g	as in good	oo	as in hood
i	as in pin	ow	as in how
		y	as in spy

Abergavenny	Aber-ga-*ven*-i (town) Aber-*gen*-i (title)	Ashburnham	*Ash*-burnam
Abinger	*Ab*-binjer	Ashburton	*Ash*-burton
Acheson	*Ach*-ison	Ashcombe	*Ash*-com
Achonry	*Acon*-ri	Assheton	*Ash*-ton
Ackroyd	*Ak*-roid	Atherton	*Ath*-erton
Agate	*Ay*-gat	Athlumney	Ath-*lum*-ni
Ailesbury	*Ayls*-bri	Atholl	*Ath*-ol
Ailsa	*Ayl*-sa	Auchinleck	*Aff*-leck *Awk*-inleck
Aitchison	*Aych*-ison		
Akerman	*Ack*-erman	Auchterlonie	*Aukh*-ter-*lōn*-i
Akers-Douglas	*Ay*-kers-*Dug*-glas	Ava	*Ah*-va
Alcester	*Aw*-ster	Ayers	Airs
Aldenham	*Awl*-dnam		
Alington	*Al*-ington	Baden-Powell	*Bay*-dn-*Pō*-ell
Alleyne	*Al*-leen, Al-*lane* *Al*-len	Bagehot	*Baj*-jut
		Baggallay	*Bag*-gali
Allhusen	Al-*hew*-sen	Balcarres	Bal-*car*-riss
Alnemouth	*Ayl*-mouth	Baldry	*Bawl*-dri
Alnwick	*An*-nick	Balfour	*Bal*-four
Alresford	*Awl*-sford	Balgonie	Bal-*gō*-ni
Althorp	*Awl*-trup	Balogh	Ballog
Altrincham	*Awl*-tringam	Bamfyld	*Bam*-feeld
Amory	A-mori	Barham	*Bah*-ram
Ampthill	*Amt*-hill	Barnardiston	Barnar-*dis*-ton
Annaly	*An*-nali	Barraclough	*Bar*-racluff
Annesley	*An*-sli	Barttelot	*Bart*-ilot
Anstruther	*An*-struther	Barwick	*Bar*-rick, also as spelt
Antrobus	*An*-trobus	Bateson	*Bayt*-son
Arbuthnott	Ar-*buth*-not	Battye	*Bat*-ti
Archdall	*Arch*-dale	Baugh	Baw
Ardagh	*Ar*-da	Beaconsfield	*Beck*-onsfield (town) *Bee*-consfield (title)
Ardee	Ar-*dee*		
Argyll	Ar-*gyle*	Beatty	*Bee*-ti
Armagh	Ar-*mah*	Beauchamp	*Bee*-cham

Beauclerc/k	*Bō*-clare
Beaufort	*Bō*-fort
Beaulieu	*Bew*-li
Beaumont	*Bō*-mont
Belisha	Be-*lee*-sha
Bellamy	*Bel*-lami
Bellew	{ *Bell*-yew / Bell-*oo*
Bellingham	{ *Bell*-injam / *Bell*-ingam
Belvoir	*Bee*-ver
Berkeley	*Bark*-li
Berkshire	*Bark*-shere
Berners	*Ber*-ners
Bertie	*Bar*-ti
Besley	{ *Beez*-li / *Bez*-li
Bessborough	*Bez*-burra
Bethune	*Bee*-ton
Bicester	*Bis*-ter
Biddulph	*Bid*-dulf
Bigelow	*Big*-gelo
Bispham	*Bis*-pam
Blakiston	*Black*-iston
Blois	Bloyce
Blomefield ⎫ Blomfield ⎬	B*loom*-field
Blount	Blunt
Blyth	{ Bly / Blyth
Bois	Boyce
Boleyn	{ *Boo*-len / *Bo*-linn
Bolingbroke	*Bol*-linbrook
Bolitho	By-*ly*-tho
Bompas	*Bum*-pas
Bonsor	*Bon*-sor
Boord	Bord
Borrowes	*Bur*-roze
Borthwick	*Borth*-wick
Bosanquet	*Bōzn*-ket
Boscawen	{ Bo-*scō*-en / Bo-*scaw*-en
Bosham	*Boz*-um
Boughey	*Bow*-i
Boughton	{ *Bow*-ton / *Baw*-ton
Bourchier	*Bow*-cher
Bourke	Berk
Bourne	{ Born / Bern / Bourn

Bowles	Boles
Brabazon	*Brab*-bazon
Brabourne	*Bray*-bn
Breadalbane	Bred-*awl*-ban
Brechin	*Breek*-hin
Broke	Brook
Brough	Bruff
Brougham	Broom
Broughton	*Braw*-ton
Buccleuch	Buckloo
Buchan	*Buk*-han
Buchanan	Bu-*can*-non
Burbury	*Ber*-bery
Burges	*Ber*-jez
Burghclere	*Ber*-clair
Burghersh	*Ber*-gersh
Burghley	*Ber*-li
Burroughes	*Bur*-roze
Bury	{ *Ber*-ri / *Bew*-ri
Caccia	Katcha
Cadogan	Ka-*dug*-gan
Cahill	*Kay*-hill
Caillard	*Ky*-ar
Caius	Kees
Calderon	*Kawld*-eron
Callaghan	{ *Kall*-ahan / *Kall*-igan
Calthorpe	*Kawl*-thorp
Camoys	Kam-*oys*
Campden	*Kam*-den
Capell	*Kay*-pel
Carbery	*Kar*-beri
Carew	{ *Kair*-i / Kar-*oo*
Carlyon	Kar-*ly*-on
Carmichael	Kar-*my*-kal
Carnegie	Kar-*neg*-gi
Carnwath	*Karn*-woth
Carpmael	*Karp*-male
Carruthers	Kar-*ruth*-ers
Carshalton	Kar-*shaw*-ton
Cassilis	*Kas*-sels
Castlereagh	*Kah*-selray
Cavan	*Kav*-van
Cavanagh	*Kav*-vana
Chalmers	*Chah*-mers
Chaloner	*Chal*-loner
Chandos	*Shan*-dos
Charlemont	*Charl*-mon

Charteris	{ *Char*-teris { *Char*-ters
Cheetham	*Cheet*-am
Cherwell	*Char*-well
Chetwode	*Chet*-wood
Chetwynd	*Chet*-wind
Cheylesmore	*Chil*-smor
Cheyne	*Chay*-ni
Chichele	{ *Chich*-eli { Chi-*chai*ley
Chisholm	*Chiz*-zom
Chiswick	*Chiz*-ik
Cholmeley Cholmondeley Chomley	*Chum*-li
Cirencester	*Syr*-ensester
Clanricarde	Klan-*rick*-ard
Clarina	Kla-*reen*-a
Claverhouse	{ *Klay*-vers, also { as spelt
Clerk	Klark
Clerke	Klark
Cliveden	*Kliv*-den
Clogher	Klo-her
Cloncurry	Klun-*cur*-ri
Clonmell	Klon-*mel*
Clough	Kluff
Clowes	{ Klews { Klows
Clwyd	*Klew*-id
Cochrane	*Kock*-ran
Cockburn	*Ko*-burn
Coghill	*Kog*-hill
Coke	{ Kook { Koke
Colborne	*Kole*-burn
Colles	*Kol*-lis
Colquhoun	Ko-*hoon*
Colville	{ *Koll*-vil { *Koal*-vil
Combe	Koom
Compton	*Kump*-ton
Conisborough	*Kun*-sbra
Constable	*Kun*-stable
Conyngham	*Kun*-ningam
Copleston	*Kop*-pelston
Corcoran	*Kork*-ran
Cottenham	*Kot*-tenam
Cottesloe	*Kot*-slo
Couch	Kōōch
Courtenay Courtney	*Kort*-ni

Courthope	*Kort*-ope
Courtown	*Kor*-town
Cousens	*Kuz*-zens
Coutts	Kōōts
Coventry	{ *Kov*-entri { *Kuv*-entri
Coverdale	*Kuv*-erdale
Coverley	*Kuv*-erli
Cowell	{ *Kow*-ell { *Kō*-ell
Cowen	{ *Kō*-en { *Kow*en
Cowles	Koles
Cowper	{ *Kōō*-per { *Kow*-per
Cozens	*Kuz*-zens
Craigavon	Craig-*a*-von
Craster	*Crah*-ster
Crawshay	*Kraw*-shay
Creagh	Kray
Creighton	*Kry*-ton
Crespigny	*Krep*-ni
Crichton	*Kry*-ton
Croghan	*Krō*-an
Cromartie	*Krum*-marti
Crombie	*Krum*-bi
Culme-Seymour	*Kulm*-*See*-mer
Cuningham Cuninghame Cunyngham	*Kun*-ningam
Dacre	*Day*-ker
Dacres	*Day*-kers
Dahrendorf	*Darr*-endorf
Dalbiac	*Dawl*-biac
Dalgleish	Dal-*gleesh*
Dalhousie	Dal-*how*-zi
Dalmeny	Dal-*men*-ni
Dalrymple	Dal-*rim*-ple
Dalziel	{ Dee-*ell* { Dal-*zeel*
Daubeney	*Daw*-bni
Daventry	As spelt
Death	De-*ath*
De Burgh	De Berg
Decies	*Dee*-shees
De Crespigny	De *Krep*-ni
De Hoghton	De Horton
De la Poer	De la Poor
De la Warr	*De*-lawar
De l'Isle	De Lyle
De Moleyns	*Dem*-moleens

De Montmorency	De Muntmor-*en*-si
Denbigh	*Den*-bi
Derby	*Dar*-bi
Dering	*Deer*-ing
De Rohan	De *Ro*-an
De Ros	De Roos
Derwent	{ *Dar*-went, also as spelt
De Salis	{ De *Sal*-lis / De Sahls
De Saumarez / De Sausmarez	De *So*-marez
Devereux	{ *Dev*-veroo / *Dev*-veroox
De Vesci	De *Vess*-i
D'Eyncourt	Dain-curt
De Zoete	De Zōōt
Dillwyn	*Dil*-lon
Disraeli	Diz-*rail*-i
Donegal	*Don*-igawl
Doneraile	*Dun*-erayl
Donoghue	*Dun*-nohoo
Donoughmore	*Dun*-nomor
Dougall	*Doo*-gal
Doughty	*Dow*-ti
Douglas	*Dug*-las
Drogheda	*Draw*-eda
Du Cane	Dew *Kane*
Duchesne	Du-*kahn*
Ducie	*Dew*-ssi
Dumaresq	Doo-*mer*-rick
Dumfries	Dum-*freess*
Dunalley	Dun-*nal*-li
Dundas	Dun-*das*
Dungarvan	Dun-*gar*-van
Dunglass	Dun-*glass*
Dunmore	Dun-*mor*
Dunsany	Dun-*sa*-ni
Duntze	Dunts
Dupplin	*Dup*-plin
Du Quesne	Dew *Kane*
Durand	Dew-*rand*
Durrant	{ Dur-*rant* / *Dur*-rant
Dwyfor	*Dwy*-for
Dymoke	*Dim*-muk
Dynevor	*Din*-nevor
Dysart	*Dy*-sart
Eardley-Wilmot	*Erd*-li-*Wil*-mot
Ebrington	*Ebb*-rington
Ebury	*Ee*-beri

Edgcumbe	*Ej*-cum
Edwardes	Edwards
Egerton	*Ej*-erton
Elam	*Ee*-lam
Elcho	*El*-ko
Elibank	*El*-libank
Eliot	*Ell*-iot
Ellesmere	*Els*-meer
Elphinstone	*El*-finston
Elwes	El-*weez*
Enniskillen	*In*-nis-*kil*-len
Ernle	*Ern*-li
Esmonde	*Ez*-mond
Etheredge	*Eth*-erij
Evershed	*Ev*-ershed
Ewart	*U*-art
Eyre	Air
Eyton	*Y*-ton
Falconbridge	*Fawk*-onbrij
Falconer	*Fawk*-ner
Falkland	*Fawk*-land
Farquhar	{ *Fark*-wer / *Fark*-er
Farquharson	{ *Fark*-werson / *Fark*-erson
Fawcett	{ *Faw*-set / *Foss*-et
Featherstonhaugh	*Feth*-erstonhaw
Feilden	*Feel*-den
Feilding	*Feel*-ding
Fenwick	*Fen*-ick
Fermanagh	*Fer*-mana
Feversham	*Fav*-ersham
Ffolkes	Fokes
Ffoulkes	{ Fokes / Fōōks
Fiennes	Fynes
Findlater	*Fin*-litter
Findlay	*Fin*-li
Fingall	*Fin*-gawl
Fitzhardinge	Fitz-*hard*-ing
Fleming	*Flem*-ming
Foljambe	*Fool*-jam
Forbes	Forbs
Fortescue	*Fort*-iskew
Foulis	Fowls
Fowey	Foy
Fowke	Foke
Freake	Freek
Fremantle	Free-*man*-tle

Freyer	*Free*-ar / *Fry*-er	Graeme	Grame
Froude	Frōōd	Graham / Grahame	*Gray*-am
Furneaux	*Fur*-no	Granard	*Gran*-nard
		Greaves	Graves / Greeves
Gairdner	*Gard*-ner		
Galbraith	Gal-*brayth*	Greenhalgh	*Green*-how / *Green*-haltch
Gallagher	*Gal*-laher	Greig	Greg
Gallwey		Greville	*Grev*-el
Galway	*Gawl*-way	Grier	Greer
Garmoyle	Gar-*moyl*	Grosvenor	*Grove*-nor
Garnock	*Gar*-nock	Guildford	*Gil*-ford
Garvagh	*Gar*-va	Guinness	*Gin*-iss
Gatacre	*Gat*-taker	Gwatkin	*Gwot*-kin
Gathorne	*Gay*-thorn	Gwynedd	*Gwin*-eth
Geddes	*Ged*-diz	Gye	Jy
Gee	Gee / Jee		
Geikie	*Gee*-ki	Haden	*Hay*-dn
Gell	Gell / Jell	Haggard	*Hag*-gard
		Haigh	Hayg
Geoghegan	*Gay*-gun	Haldane	*Hawl*-dane
Gerard	*Jer*-rard	Haldon	*Hawl*-don
Gervis-Meyrick	*Jer*-vis-*Mer*-ick	Hallé	*Hal*-lay
Gethen / Gethin / Gething	*Geth*-in / *Geeth*-in	Halsbury	*Hawl*-sbri
		Halsey	*Hawl*-si / *Hal*-si
Gibbes	Gibbs		
Giddens	*Gid*-dens	Hamond	*Ham*-mond
Giffard	*Gif*-fard / *Jif*-fard	Hampden	*Ham*-den
		Hanbury	*Han*-buri
Gilhooly	Gil-*hoo*-li	Harberton	*Har*-berton
Gilkes	Jilks	Harcourt	*Har*-curt
Gill	Gill / Jill	Hardinge	*Har*-ding
		Harewood	*Har*-wood
Gilles	*Gill*-is	Harington	*Ha*-rington
Gillespie	Gill-*ess*-pi	Harlech	*Har*-lick
Gillingham	*Jill*-ingam (Kent) / *Gill*-ingam (Dorset)	Hawarden	*Hay*-warden / *Har*-den
Gilmour	*Gil*-mor	Headlam	*Hed*-lam
Gilroy	*Gil*-roy	Heathcote	*Heth*-cot
Glamis	Glahms	Hegarty	*Heg*-arti
Glerawly	Gler-*aw*-li	Heneage	*Hen*-ij
Goldsworthy	*Gōls*-worthi	Hennessey / Hennessy	*Hen*-essi
Gomme	Gom		
Gorges	*Gor*-jiz	Henniker	*Hen*-iker
Gormanston	*Gor*-manston	Henriques	Hen-*reek*-iz
Goschen	*Gō*-shen	Hepburn	*Heb*-burn
Gough	Goff	Herries	*Her*-ris
Goulburn	*Gōōl*-burn	Herschell	*Her*-shel
Gourley	*Goor*-li	Hertford	*Har*-ford
Gower	Gaw, also as spelt	Hervey	*Her*-vi / *Har*-vi

Heytesbury	*Hayt*-sburi	Jolliffe	*Joll*-if
Hindlip	*Hind*-lip	Julyan	*Jōō*-lian
Hobart	*Hō*-bart / *Hub*-bart		
		Kaberry	*Kay*-berry
Holbech	*Hol*-beech	Keatinge	*Keet*-ing
Holmes	Homes	Keighley	*Keeth*-li
Holmesdale	*Home*-sdale	Keightley	*Keet*-li
Holm-Patrick	Home-Patrick	Keiller	*Kee*-ler
Home	Hume, also as spelt	Kekewich	*Keck*-wich
Honyman	*Hun*-niman	Kennard	Ken-ard
Honywood	*Hun*-niwood	Kenyon	*Ken*-ion
Hopetoun	*Hope*-ton	Keogh	
Hotham	*Huth*-am	Keough	*Kee*-ō
Hough	Huff	Kehoe	
Houghton	Huf-ton / *Haw*-ton / *How*-ton / *Ho*-ton	Kesteven	*Kest*-even
		Keynes	Kaynes / Keens
Houston	*Hoost*-on	Killanin	Kill-*an*-in
Howorth	*How*-erth	Kilmorey	Kil-*mur*-ri
Hugessen	*Hew*-jessen / *Hew*-gessen	Kincairney	Kin-*cair*-ni
		Kingscote	*Kings*-cut
Huish	*Hew*-ish	Kinnaird	Kin-*naird*
Humphrey	*Hum*-fri	Kinnear	Kin-*near*
Hunstanton	*Hun*-ston, or as spelt	Kinnoull	Kin-*nool*
Hyndman	*Hynd*-man	Kirkcudbright	Kirk-*oo*-bri
		Knightly	*Nyt*-ly
		Knighton	*Ny*-ton
Iddesleigh	*Id*-sli	Knollys	
Ightham	*Y*-tam	Knowles	Noles
Inchiquin	*Inch*-quin	Knutsford	*Nuts*-ford
Inge	Ing	Kynaston	*Kin*-naston
Ingelow	*In*-jelow		
Ingestre	*In*-gestri	Lacon	*Lay*-kon
Ingham	*Ing*-am	Laffan	La-*ffan*
Inglis	*In*-gools, or as spelt	Langrishe	*Lang*-rish
Innes	*In*-nis	Larpent	*Lar*-pent
Inveraray	Inver-*air*-i	Lascelles	*Las*-sels
Inverarity	Inver-*arr*-iti	Lathom	*Lay*-thom
Isitt	*Y*-sit	Laughton	*Law*-ton
Iveagh	*Y*-va	Lavengro	*Lav*-engro
		Lawrence	*Lor*-rence
Jacoby	*Jack*-obi	Layard	Laird, or as spelt
Jeaffreson	*Jeff*-erson	Lea	Lee
Jeffreys	*Jef*-riz	Learmonth	*Ler*-munth
Jerome	Jer-*ome*	Leatham	*Leeth*-am
Jervaulx	*Jer*-vis	Leathes	Leeths / *Leeth*-iz
Jervis	Jar-vis / Jer-vis	Lechmere	*Leech*-meer
Jervois	*Jar*-vis	Leconfield	*Lek*-onfield
Jeune	Joon	Le Fanu	*Leff*-enyu / *Leff*-noo
Jeyes	Jays		
Jocelyn	*Joss*-lin	Lefevre	Le-*fee*-ver

Lefroy	Le-*froy*	M'Culloch	Ma-*cul*-lokh
Legard	*Lej*-ard	M'Eachern	Mac-*kek*-run
Legge	Leg	McEvoy	*Mack*-evoy
Legh	Lee	M'Ewan ⎱	
Lehmann	*Lay*-man	MacEwen ⎰	Mac-*kew*-an
Leicester	*Lest*-er	M'Gee ⎱	
Leigh	Lee	M'Ghee ⎰	Ma-*gee*
Leighton	*Lay*-ton	MacGillivray	Ma-*gil*-veri
Leinster	⎰ Len-ster	M'Gillycuddy	*Mack*-licuddi
	⎱ *Lin*-ster	Machell	*May*-chell
Leishman	*Leesh*-man	Machen	*May*-chen
Leitrim	*Leet*-rim	M'Illwraith	*Mack*-ilrayth
Lemesurier	Le-*méz*urer	MacIver ⎱	
Leominster	*Lem*-ster	M'Ivor ⎰	Mack-y-ver
Le Patourel	Le-*pat*-turel	McKay	Mac-*ky*
Le Poer	Le-*por*	Mackie	*Mack*-i
Le Queux	Le *Kew*	Maclachlan	Mac-*laukh*-lan
Leven	*Lee*-ven	Maclagan	Mac-*lag*-gan
Leverhulme	*Lee*-verhewm	Maclaren	Mac-*lar*-ren
Leveson-Gower	*Lōō*-son-Gaw	Maclean	Ma-*clayn*
Levey	⎰ *Lee*-vi	Macleay	Ma-*clay*
	⎱ *Lev*-vi	Macleod	Ma-*clowd*
Ley	Lee	Macmahon	⎰ Mac-*mahn* (with
Leyland	*Lay*-land		⎱ internal h)
Liardet	*Lee*-ardet	Macnamara	Macna-*mah*-ra
Lingen	*Ling*-en	M'Naught	Mac-*nawt*
Lisle	⎰ Lyle	MacNaughton	Mac-*naw*-ton
	⎱ Leel	Macneill	Mac-*neel*
Listowel	Lis-*tō*-el	Maconchy	Ma-*conk*-i
Llangattock	Klan-*gat*-tock	Maconochie	Mack-*on*-okhi
Llewellyn	Loo-*ell*-in	Magdalen(e)	*Mawd*-lin
Lochiel	Lok-*heel*	Magrath	Ma-*grah*
Logue	Lōg	Maguire	Ma-*gwire*
Lough	Luff	Mahon	⎰ Mahn
Loughborough	*Luf*-burra		⎱ Ma-*hoon*
Lovat	*Luv*-at	Mahony	⎰ *Mah*-ni
Lovibond	⎰ *Luv*-band, also as		⎱ Ma-hōn-i
	⎱ spelt	Mainwaring	*Man*-nering
Lowther	*Low*-ther	Majendie	*Maj*-endi
Lugard	Loo-*gard*	Malet	*Mal*-let
Lygon	*Lig*-gon	Mall, The	Mal, The
Lymington	*Lim*-mington	Malmesbury	*Mahm*-sbri
Lympne	Lim	Mansergh	*Man*-zer
Lynam	*Ly*-nam	Marjoribanks	*March*-banks
Lysaght	*Ly*-sat or *Ly*-sacht	Marlborough	*Mawl*-bra
Lysons	*Ly*-sons	Martineau	*Mart*-ino
Lyveden	*Liv*-den	Masham	*Mass*-am
		Maskelyne	*Mask*-elin
Macalister	Mac-*al*-ister	Massereena	Ma*zereena*
Macara	Mac-*ah*-ra	Mather	⎰ *May*-ther
McCorquodale	Ma-*cork*-odale		⎱ *Math*-er
Maccullagh	Ma-*cul*-la		

Matheson	{ *Math*-ison { *Mat*-tison
Maugham	Mawm
Maughan	Mawn
Maunsell	*Man*-sell
Maurice	*Mor*-ris
Mayo	*May*-o
Meath	Meeth
Meiklejohn	*Mick*-eljon
Meldrum	*Mel*-drum
Melhuish	*Mel*-lish
Menzies	{ *Meng*-iz { *Menz*-iz { *Ming*-iz
Meopham	{ *Mep*-am { *Meff*-am
Mereworth	*Merri*-worth
Meux	Mewz
Meyer	*My*-er
Meynell	*Men*-nel
Meyrick	*Mer*-rick
Meysey-Thompson	*May*-zi-*Toms*-on
Michelham	*Mich*-lam
Michie	*Mik*-ki
Midleton	Middleton
Mildmay	*Myld*-may
Millard	Mil-*lard*
Milles	Mills
Milngavie	Mull-*gy*
Molyneaux } Molyneux }	{ *Mol*-neux { *Mol*-new
Monaghan	*Mon*-nahan
Monck	Munk
Monckton	*Munk*-ton
Moncrieff	Mon-*creef*
Monkhouse	*Munk*-hows
Monkswell	*Munk*-swell
Monro } Monroe }	Mun-*ro*
Monson	*Mun*-son
Montagu	*Mont*-agew
Monteagle	Mun-*tee*-gle
Montefiore	Montifi-*or*-i
Montgomery	Munt-*gum*-meri
Monzie	Mun-*ee*
Moran	*Mor*-an
Morant	Mo-*rant*
Moray	*Mur*-ri
Mordaunt	*Mor*-dunt
Morice	*Mor*-ris
Morrell	Murr-ell
Mostyn	*Moss*-tin

Mouat	*Moo*-at
Moule	Mole
Moulton	*Mōl*-ton
Mountmorres	Mount-*mor*-ris
Mowat	{ *Mo*-at { *Moo*-at
Mowbray	{ *Mow*-bri { *Moo*-bri
Moynihan	*Moy*-ni-han
Muncaster	*Mun*-kaster
Naas	Nace
Naesmyth	*Nay*-smith
Napier	*Nay*-pier
Neave	Neev
Neil	Neel
Nepean	Ne-*peen*
Newburgh	*New*-bra
Newnes	Newns
Nigel	*Ny*-jel
Niven	*Niv*-ven
Northbourne	*North*-burn
Northcote	*North*-cot
Nunburnholme	Nun-*bern*-um
O'Callaghan	*Ocall*-ahan
Ochterlony	Octerl-*o*-ni
O'Donoghue	O-*dun*-nahoo
Ogilvy	O-gelvi
O'Hagan	O-*hay*-gan
Olivier	{ O-*liv*-vier { O-*liv*-iay
O'Meara	O-*mah*-ra
O'Morchoe	O-*mur*-roo
Onions	{ O-*ny*-ons { *Un*-ions
Ormonde	*Or*-mond
Osbourne	*Os*-burn
O'Shaughnessy	{ O-*shaw*-nessi { O-*shawk*-nessi
Outram	*Oo*tram
Paget	*Paj*-it
Pakenham	*Pack*-enum
Palgrave	Pal-grave
Parnell	*Par*-nal
Pasley	*Pay*-zli
Paterson	*Pat*-terson
Paton	*Pay*-ton
Pauncefote	*Powns*-foot
Pease	Peez
Pechell	*Pee*-chel

Pembroke	*Pem*-brook	Ranfurly	*Ran*-ferli
Pennefather	*Pen*-nifether	Ranjitsinhji	*Ran*-jit-*sin*-ji
Pennycuick	{ *Pen*-nicook { *Pen*-niquick	Rankeillour	Rankiller
		Rashleigh	*Rash*-li
Penrhyn	Pen-*rin*	Rathdonnell	Rath-*don*-nel
Pepys	{ Peeps (ancient) { *Pep*-piss (modern)	Rathmore	Rath-*mor*
		Rayleigh	*Ray*-li
Pery	*Peer*-i	Raynham	*Rain*-am
Peto	*Pee*-tō	Reading	*Red*-ing
Petre	*Pee*-ter	Reay	Ray
Petrie	*Pee*-tri	Renwick	*Ren*-nick
Pierpoint }	{ Peerpont, also as	Reuter	*Roy*-ter
Pierrepoint }	{ spelt	Rhondda	*Ron*-tha
Pigou	Pi-*goo*	Rhys	{ Rees { Rice
Pirbright	*Per*-brite		
Pirie	Pirri	Riddell	*Rid*-dle
Pleydell-Bouverie	*Pled*-el *Boo*-veri	Rievaulx	{ *Riv*-els { *Reev*-o
Pochin	*Putch*-in		
Pole	{ Pool { Pōl	Robartes	Ro-*barts*
		Roche	Roche
Pole Carew	Pool *Cair*-i	Rolleston	*Rol*-ston
Poltimore	*Pol*-timor	Romilly	*Rom*-ili
Polwarth	*Pole*-werth	Romney	{ *Rum*-ni { *Rom*-ni
Ponsonby	*Pun*-sunbi		
Pontefract	{ *Pum*-fret, also as { spelt	Ronaldshay	*Ron*-ald-shay
		Rothes	*Roth*-is
Portal	*Por*-tal	Rothwell	*Row*-ell
Porteous	*Por*-tius	Rouse	Rouse
Poulett	*Pau*-let	Routh	Rowth
Powell	{ *Po*-ell { *Pow*-ell	Roxburghe	*Rox*-bra
		Ruislip	*Ry*-slip
Powerscourt	*Poor*-scort	Ruthven	{ *Riv*-ven { *Ri*-then
Powlett	*Paw*-let		
Powys	*Po*-is	Sacheverell	Sash-*ev*-erel
Praed	Prade	St. Aubyn	S'nt *Aw*-bin
Pretyman	*Prit*-timan	St. Clair	*Sin*-clair
Prevost	*Prev*-vo	St. Cyres	Sin-*seer*
Prideaux	{ *Pree*-do { *Prid*-dux { *Prid*-do	St. John	*Sin*-jun
		St. Leger	{ *Sil*-linjer { S'nt *Lej*-er
Probyn	*Pro*-bin	St. Maur	{ S'nt Mor { *See*-mer
Prothero	*Proth*-ero		
Prowse	Prowz	St. Neots	S'nt *Neets*
Pugh	Pew	Salisbury	*Sawl*-sberri
Pwellheli	*Pool*-helli	Saltoun	{ *Sawl*-ton { *Sal*-ton
Pytchley	*Pych*-li		
		Sandes } Sandys }	Sands
Ralegh	{ *Raw*-li { *Ral*-li	Sault-St. Marie	*Soo*-St. Marie
		Saumarez } Sausmarez }	{ *So*-marrez { *Sum*-mers
Ralph	{ Ralf { Rafe		
Ranelagh	*Ran*-ela	Saunders	*Sahn*-ders

Saunderson	*Sahn*-derson	Sudley	*Sud*-li
Saye and Sele	Say an Seel	Suirdale	*Sheur*-dale
Sayer	Sair	Sweatman	Swet-man
Scafell	{ *Scaw*-fell { *Scah*-fell	Sweetman	*Sweet*-man
		Symonds	*Sim*-monds
Scarborough	*Scar*-burra	Symons	{ *Sim*-mons, also as { spelt
Scarbrough	*Scar*-bra		
Sclater	*Slay*-ter	Synge	Sing
Scone	Scoon		
Scrymgeour	*Scrim*-jer	Tangye	*Tang*-i
Searle	Serl	Teignmouth	*Tin*-muth
Sedbergh	*Sed*-ber	Tewkesbury	*Tewks*-berri
Sempill	*Semp*-il	Teynham	*Tan*-am
Sergeant	*Sar*-jent	Thames	Tems
Seton } Setoun }	*See*-ton	Theobald	*Tib*-bald, also as spelt
		Thesiger	*Thes*-sijer
Seymour	{ *See*-mer { *See*-mor	Thorold	{ *Thur*-uld, also as { spelt
Shakerley	*Shak*-erli	Thuillier	*Twil*-lier
Shearman	*Sher*-man	Thynne	Thin
Sherborne	{ *Sher*-bern { *Sher*-born	Tighe	Ty
		Tollemache	*Tol*-mash
Shrewsbury	*Shrō*-sberri	Torphichen	Tor-*fick*-en
Sidebotham	*Side*-bottam	Toynbee	*Toyn*-bi
Skrine	Skreen	Trafalgar	{ Tra-*fal*-gar (Square) { Trafal-*gar* (title)
Slaithwaite	*Slo*-it, also as spelt		
Smijth	Smythe	Traquair	Trak-*ware*
Sodor	*So*-dor	Tredegar	Tred-*ee*-gar
Somers	*Sum*-mers	Trefusis	Tre-*few*-sis
Somerset	*Sum*-erset	Treloar	Tre-*lor*
Somerton	*Sum*-merton	Trevelyan	Tre-*vi*-lian
Sondes	Sonds	Trewin	Tre-*win*
Sotherby	*Suth*-ebi	Trimlestown	*Trim*-melston
Southwell	*Su*-thell	Troubridge	*Troo*-bridge
Speight	Spate	Tuite	Tewt
Stalbridge	*Stawl*-bridge	Tullibardine	Tulli-*bard*-een
Stanton	*Stahn*-ton	Turnour	*Ter*-ner
Stavordale	*Stay*-vordale	Tyrwhitt	*Tir*-rit
Stormonth	*Stor*-munth	Tyssen	*Ty*-sen
Stoughton	{ Staw-ton { Stow-ton	Tytler	*Tyt*-ler
Stourton	*Ster*-ton	Uist	*Oo*-ist
Strachan	*Strack*-en	Urquhart	*Erk*-ert
Strachey	*Stray*-chi	Uttoxeter	Yew-*tox*-eter
Strahan	Strawn		
Stranraer	Stran-*rar*	Vanburgh	*Van*-bra
Strathallan	Strath-*al*-an	Van Dyck	Van-*dyke*
Strathcona	Strath-*co*-na	Van Straubenzee	Van Straw-*ben*-zie
Stratheden	Strath-*ee*-den	Vaughan	Vawn
Strathmore	*Strath*-mor	Vaux	{ Vox { Vokes
Stucley	*Stew*-kli		
Sudeley	*Sewd*-li	Vavasour	*Vav*-vaser

Vesey	*Vee*-zi	Wroughton	*Raw*-ton
Villiers	*Vil*-lers	Wylie	
Vyvyan	*Viv*-vian	Wyllie }	*Wȳ*-li
Waldegrave	*Wawl*-grave	Yeates	Yayts
Waleran	*Wawl*-ran	Yeatman	*Yayt*-man
Walford	*Wawl*-ford	Yeats	Yayts
Wallop	*Wol*-lup	Yerburgh	*Yar*-burra
Walmesley	*Wawm*-sli	Yonge	Yung
Walsingham	*Wawl*-singam		
Wantage	*Won*-tij	Zouche	Zoosh
Warburton	*War*-burton		
Warre	Wor		
Warwick	*Wor*-rick		
Wauchope	*Waw*-kup		
Waugh	Waw		
Wednesbury	*Wens*-berri		
Weir	Weer		
Wellesley	{ *Wel*-sli / *Wes*-li }		
Wemyss	Weems		
Westcott	*West*-cot		
Westenra	*West*-enra		
Whalley	*Whay*-li		
Wilde	Wyld		
Willard	Will-*ard*		
Willes	Wills		
Willoughby	*Wil*-lobi		
Willoughby-D'Eresby	*Wil*-lobi-Dersbi		
Willoughby de Broke	*Wil*-loby de Brook		
Winchilsea	*Winch*-elsee		
Winstanley	*Win*-stanli		
Woburn	*Woo*-bern		
Wodehouse	*Wood*-house		
Wolcombe	*Wool*-cum		
Wollaston	*Wool*-aston		
Wolmer	*Wool*-mer		
Wolseley	*Wool*-sli		
Wombwell	*Woom*-well		
Woolwich	*Wool*-ich		
Worcester	*Woos*-ter		
Worsley	*Wer*-sli		
Wortley	*Wert*-li		
Wraxhall	*Rax*-all		
Wreford	*Ree*-ford		
Wrey	Ray		
Wriothesley	{ *Ry*-othsli / *Rox*-li }		
Wrixon	*Rix*-on		
Wrotham	{ *Roo*-tham / *Root*-em }		
Wrottesley	*Rot*-sli		

Index